Copyright © 2025 by Artemus Tanner

All rights reserved.

No portion of this book may be reproduced in any form without written permission from the publisher or author, except as permitted by U.S. copyright law.

Disclaimer

This text is for educational and inspirational purposes, not a substitute for professional medical or psychological advice. If you have concerns about your mental or physical health, seek qualified care. Always adapt techniques to your comfort level and consult professionals when needed.

Stress Less, Live More

A Mindful Path to Instant Anxiety Relief and Emotional Resilience

Artemus Tanner

Table of Contents

FOREWORD 7

CHAPTER 1 FACING THE STRESS MONSTER
    INTRODUCTION 23
    1.1 THE REALITIES OF STRESS 26
    1.2 RECOGNIZING YOUR PATTERNS 30
    1.3 SETTING THE STAGE FOR GROWTH 34

CHAPTER 2 MINDSET SHIFT 101
    INTRODUCTION 42
    2.1 BREAKING MENTAL BARRIERS 44
    2.2 ADOPTING A GROWTH MINDSET 49
    2.3 SEEING OBSTACLES AS OPPORTUNITIES 54

CHAPTER 3 EMBRACING THE IMPERFECTIONS
    INTRODUCTION 62
    3.1 WHY FLAWS MAKE US HUMAN 64
    3.2 LETTING GO OF PERFECTIONISM 68
    3.3 FINDING PEACE IN ACCEPTANCE 72

CHAPTER 4 BREATHE, RELAX, REPEAT
    INTRODUCTION 81
    4.1 SIMPLE BREATHING HACKS 84
    4.2 CREATING A DAILY RELAXATION RITUAL 89
    4.3 QUICK TENSION RELEASE TECHNIQUES 94

CHAPTER 5 MINDFUL MOMENTS
    INTRODUCTION 101
    5.1 OBSERVING THOUGHTS WITHOUT JUDGMENT 103
    5.2 CULTIVATING MINDFUL HABITS 107
    5.3: GRATITUDE AS A GAME-CHANGER 112

CHAPTER 6 MASTERING EMOTIONAL WAVES
- INTRODUCTION 119
- 6.1 IDENTIFYING EMOTIONAL TRIGGERS 121
- 6.2 RIDING THE UPS AND DOWNS 126
- 6.3: EMOTIONAL RESILIENCE TACTICS 131

CHAPTER 7 HEALTHY BOUNDARIES, HAPPY LIFE
- INTRODUCTION 138
- 7.1 LEARNING TO SAY "NO" 140
- 7.2 RESPECTING YOUR OWN LIMITS 145
- 7.3 SOCIAL INTERACTIONS WITHOUT BURNOUT 151

CHAPTER 8 NOURISH YOUR BODY, NOURISH YOUR SOUL
- INTRODUCTION 160
- 8.1 STRESS-LESS EATING HABITS 162
- 8.2 THE POWER OF MOVEMENT 166
- 8.3 RESTFUL SLEEP ESSENTIALS 170

CHAPTER 9 PRODUCTIVE WITHOUT THE PRESSURE
- INTRODUCTION 176
- 9.1 TIME MANAGEMENT BASICS 178
- 9.2 FOCUS AND FLOW 183
- 9.3 GENTLE ACCOUNTABILITY 187

CHAPTER 10 CULTIVATING SELF-COMPASSION
- INTRODUCTION 195
- 10.1 POSITIVE SELF-TALK 198
- 10.2 FORGIVING YOUR PAST 203
- 10.3 CELEBRATING SMALL WINS 207

CHAPTER 11 BUILDING INNER ENERGY
- INTRODUCTION 215
- 11.1 FINDING YOUR FUEL 217
- 11.2 PROTECTING YOUR VIBE 222
- 11.3 RECHARGING FOR GROWTH 226

CHAPTER 12 FINDING MOMENTS OF JOY

    INTRODUCTION 233
    12.1 MINI-BREAK ADVENTURES 235
    12.2 JOY JOURNALING 239
    12.3 THE POWER OF PLAY 243

CHAPTER 13 CONNECTING WITH OTHERS

    INTRODUCTION 249
    13.1 SUPPORT NETWORKS 251
    13.2 PRACTICING EMPATHY 255
    13.3 NURTURING YOUR RELATIONSHIPS 259

CHAPTER 14 GROWING THROUGH CHALLENGE

    INTRODUCTION 265
    14.1 TURNING SETBACKS INTO STEPPING STONES 267
    14.2 BUILDING RESILIENCE MUSCLES 271
    14.3 KEEPING THE MOMENTUM 275

CHAPTER 15 LIVING IN FULLNESS

    INTRODUCTION 282
    15.1 HONORING YOUR JOURNEY 284
    15.2 SUSTAINING PEACE AND LOVE 288
    15.3 ONGOING EVOLUTION 292

AFTERWORD 299

BIBLIOGRAPHY

FOREWORD

A Gentle Invitation

Welcome to what may well be the beginning of a gentler, more enriching chapter in your life.

You're standing at the threshold of a book that promises something extraordinary: the possibility of **stressing less** while **living more**—a profound concept that, ironically, can sound both entirely doable and wildly out of reach.

Suppose you've wondered why daily existence feels like a marathon you never entirely signed up for. In that case, this book might just become your new companion, whispering that there's another way.

You can take a moment right now to let those words sink in. It's okay to sigh quietly and think, *"Yes, maybe there's hope for me, too."*

Because, in truth, no one is inherently doomed to a life overburdened by stress, anxiety, or the nagging fear that you're forever playing catch-up. We can all discover ways to transform the heaviness into a lighter, more complimentary, playful approach to being alive.

Let me ask you directly: Are you tired of carrying tension in your shoulders, wrestling with your to-do list, and wondering if you're missing out on something more meaningful?

Do you ever fantasize about a more straightforward, sunnier routine that feels kinder, calmer, and more in tune with your heartfelt desires?

If so, you're in the right place. And if not, well, maybe you're here simply out of curiosity: *"Could I learn something useful from these pages?"* Absolutely yes.

This book isn't just about handling stress; it's about reclaiming the joy in every day's small moments—whether it's that warm sip of coffee, a heartfelt laugh with a friend, or the sunset that splashes color across the evening sky.

It's about turning ordinary living into a blend of calm, connection, and quiet excitement for what's possible.

You might feel a blend of eagerness and skepticism. That's natural. After all, books on personal growth, mindfulness, and anxiety reduction aren't exactly rare. The world is teeming with advice—from social media soundbites to the neighbor on a yoga-teacher track.

But give this text a chance to reveal its heart. It's grounded in the real, sometimes messy experiences we all share, peppered with practical exercises and genuine acknowledgment that life isn't one-size-fits-all.

You'll encounter techniques that cater to both novices (perhaps you, if you've never tried meditating or journaling) and more seasoned explorers of stress management.

You'll glean insights for personal reflection, relational well-being, and those stumbles we all face, where everything feels like it's unraveling at the edges.

This book, "Stress Less, Live More—A Mindful Path to Instant Anxiety Relief and Emotional Resilience," will give you an integrated map of sorts, guiding you through self-discovery, mindful practice, healthy boundaries, compassion, and beyond.

But let's be clear: we don't claim to be the ultimate authority over your life. Your life experiences, distinctive quirks, and emotional mosaic are uniquely your own.

Think of these chapters as a series of supportive frameworks—windows flung open to let in fresh air, so your path can be illuminated by new, encouraging perspectives. In that sense, every reader's journey with this book is uniquely theirs.

You might adopt specific tools wholeheartedly, set others aside for later, or tweak them to fit your daily reality. That's exactly how it should be.

So let this be your gentle invitation: approach these pages with an open mind. Let curiosity lead you. Allow yourself a little vulnerability as you read, trusting that you're on the brink of a more balanced, loving, vibrant existence.

As we begin, envision yourself stepping into a sunlit clearing. In this place, your anxieties can soften, your shoulders can relax, and your mind can roam free.

Here, stress meets creativity, tension meets acceptance, and together, we'll craft a lived experience that resonates with hope and possibility.

Why This Book, Why Now?

Perhaps you're standing at a crossroads, feeling that life has become too stuffed with obligations, digital notifications, and societal pressures to hustle or do more.

Or maybe you've sensed a gaping emptiness in your day-to-day, a longing for peace so deep it's almost tangible. If you relate to any of this, know you're not alone.

We live in an age where stress almost feels like a status symbol—"I'm so busy" often equates to "I'm so important." But are we genuinely thriving in this chase?

Something within you might already be whispering that success and serenity don't have to cancel each other out. You can pursue accomplishments, yes, but do so with grace and calmness that wards off the gnawing anxiety many of us accept as "normal."

This is where the material in this book steps in. It's timely because stress, burnout, and mental fatigue have never been more prevalent—or more openly discussed.

We collectively realize the old "just push harder" mentality is unsustainable. People break under that weight, relationships fracture, and health issues crop up when we ignore our emotional well-being for too long.

Yet, it's not just about mental health in a clinical sense; it's about living a fulfilling life. Stress can dull our capacity for joy, creativity, and meaningful connections.

Think of the times you were so wound up that even a beautiful moment—a child's laughter, a friend's smile, a culinary delight—barely registered in your awareness.

That's the real tragedy: stress not only harms us physically and mentally, but it also steals the small wonders that color our existence.

So yes, the relevance of "Stress Less, Live More" is striking.

The reason to read it *now* is that it meets a deep collective and personal need: the need to reclaim our breath, to recenter our hearts, and to flourish in a world that often demands constant busyness.

The chapters within are designed to guide you step by step, layering practical strategies, reflective exercises, and heartfelt stories that demystify the process of unraveling stress.

Change can be simpler than your anxious mind imagines, especially if approached incrementally, with humor and self-compassion. Because let's face it: if you can't occasionally laugh at the absurdity of modern life, you might drown in it.

But let's also acknowledge that fundamental transformation takes time, effort, and a willingness to engage with vulnerability.

This book doesn't promise you a magical, overnight cure-all. Instead, it offers a realistic path brimming with hope—even on days when you backslide into worry, you can pick yourself up and keep going.

Each chapter will remind you that you're never beyond redemption, never too late to learn a fresh approach, never so stuck that a gentle pivot isn't possible.

A Lighthearted Approach to Deep Topics

Don't let the gravity of stress and anxiety fool you into thinking that this book will be all solemn introspection.

We believe that humor, lightness, and the occasional self-ironic smile are powerful solvents of tension.

Yes, we'll talk about hard stuff: the times you collapse onto your bed at night, feeling you've barely survived the day, or the moments anxiety slaps you awake at 3 a.m.

But we'll also talk about the comedic slip-ups—like trying that morning meditation only to realize you were so groggy you nearly fell back asleep, or that cringe-worthy moment you tried to "be mindful" in front of your friends and mixed your words embarrassingly.

Humor doesn't invalidate your struggles; it keeps you from drowning in them. Plus, it invites a playfulness that helps you explore new strategies without fear of failure.

Suppose you can laugh at yourself a bit. In that case, you're more likely to be gentle when you miss a day of journaling or forget to do your breathing exercises during a hectic lunch break.

The "live more" concept hinges partly on rediscovering your capacity for joy, spontaneity, and curiosity. Where seriousness might pin you down, humor can lift you up.

So expect some levity. You might stumble upon anecdotes about mishaps in yoga class or confessions of the author's comedic tangles with procrastination. Why? Because life is too short to approach self-help with a stiff upper lip.

We'll be honest about the messy, sometimes hilarious ways humans try to better themselves. In doing so, we lower the stakes. You're allowed to be a beginner, allowed to be imperfect.

In fact, your imperfections are what keep life interesting and keep your potential for growth wide open.

Practicing Exercises and Developing Your Talents

It's not enough to read about stress management; you have to practice it, just like you would practice a musical instrument or a new sport.

Each chapter of this book is sprinkled with exercises—some straightforward, like short breathing meditations, and others more elaborate, like journaling prompts, boundary-setting dialogues, or mini-break adventures.

These exercises are your backstage passes to real, tangible improvement. They help you turn theory into reality and concepts into muscle memory.

But let's be honest: practice can be intimidating, especially if you're juggling ten other responsibilities. You might think, *"I barely have time to do the basics—how can I fit in journaling or mindfulness, too?"*

The trick is to start small and aim for consistency rather than perfection. Could you steal five minutes in the morning or at bedtime to reflect? Could you integrate a quick breathing exercise into your lunch routine? Could you doodle your thoughts about stress on a scrap of paper while waiting for your coffee to brew? These micro-commitments repeated daily, accumulate into significant shifts over time.

Moreover, these practices aren't just about stress per se. They're also about developing your inherent talents—those relational, emotional, and creative gifts you might have neglected because you were too busy or frazzled.

For instance, journaling isn't simply a method to manage worry; it's also a tool that can unleash your storytelling flair or sharpen your self-expression.

Empathy exercises don't just defuse conflict; they enhance your emotional intelligence, improving relationships in ways that can lead to unexpected opportunities and deeper connections.

Indeed, stress management and talent development often go hand in hand. When you're less weighed down by anxiety, your mind finds space for creativity, problem-solving, and compassion.

You become more open to learning new skills, whether painting, public speaking, or a team sport. So, suppose you want to multiply your talents. In that case, one of the best ways is to free your mind from the chronic tension that suffocates curiosity.

The exercises in this book are specifically crafted to help you do just that—one step at a time, one slight shift leading to more considerable transformations.

Engaging the Reader: A Conversation, Not a Lecture

Let's be clear: this book isn't meant to be a lecture from on high, telling you how to live your life.

Think of it more like a meandering conversation with a friend—one who truly cares about your well-being and has some insights to share but also respects that you are the ultimate authority on your own experiences.

The chapters pose many questions—sometimes rhetorical, sometimes practical. That's deliberate. We want you to reflect, not just passively absorb.

So, yes, you might find yourself pausing mid-paragraph to muse over a question like, *"When was the last time I truly felt at ease?"* or *"Could I handle that next family gathering differently?"*

Embrace these pauses. Answer them if you feel prompted. If you'd instead let them marinate in the back of your mind, that's fine, too. The key is that you're not just reading; you're participating.

You're letting the material interact with the swirl of your internal world, prodding at your assumptions, gently guiding you to discover your own truths.

Because real, lasting progress thrives on personal engagement. It's like planting a seed: the text provides the water and nutrients as concepts, but you, the reader, supply the soil and the continuous care.

Without your willingness to engage, the seed remains dormant. With your open-hearted curiosity, that seed can flourish into a lovely, resilient plant that you can cultivate in your everyday life.

Addressing the "But My Life Is Specially Complicated" Thought

If you suddenly think, *"This is all well and good, but the author doesn't know how complicated my situation is,"* I hear you.

Life can get messy in ways that no general advice can fully encapsulate—whether you're juggling a demanding job, a chronic illness, multiple caregiving roles, or a swirl of conflicting obligations. This book won't pretend to have a magic wand for every nuance. But it does offer adaptable frameworks.

The examples, exercises, and perspectives aim to be flexible enough that you can calibrate them to your unique reality.

You can't devote 30 minutes a day to silent meditation. Still, you might snatch three minutes at lunchtime for a micro mindfulness session.

You may not be able to afford a weekend retreat, but you can give yourself a 10-minute mental spa break each evening with a warm beverage and a journal.

You can't fix your entire life's complexity overnight. Still, you can incorporate small changes that gradually transform your daily emotional climate. The complexity of your life does not negate the potential for meaningful, if incremental, improvements.

And yes, some complexities may warrant professional support—therapists, counselors, or specific programs that address trauma, addiction, or deep-rooted mental health issues.

While this book offers a broad toolkit, it doesn't replace specialized care. Recognizing when you need that extra layer of help is a profound act of self-respect, not a failure.

The more you read, the more you hone your instincts about what level of support your unique journey calls for.

So rest assured: You can be complicated, but you can still find ways to integrate these teachings to benefit you.

Envisioning the Benefits

If you need a little boost of motivation, let's imagine the potential outcomes of applying these chapters to your life.

Picture waking up in the morning, and instead of dread or frantic thoughts, you greet the day with a mild sense of curiosity—*"I wonder what positive thing might surprise me today?"*

Or think of finishing a stressful phone call without that familiar knot in your stomach because you've learned to regulate your breathing and reframe tension.

Visualize returning home from work and not snapping at your loved ones because you've identified your emotional triggers and practiced boundaries that let you decompress healthily.

Over time, these changes accumulate. Stress becomes an event, not a constant. Your emotional resilience grows.

You develop a friendlier rapport with yourself, dropping some of the self-criticism that used to weigh you down.

And that, in turn, liberates a portion of your brain to explore your talents, whether writing, painting, playing an instrument, or excelling in your field.

You realize less stress equals more bandwidth for creativity, relationships, and meaningful experiences.

That's the essence of living more: not necessarily doing more in quantity but embracing more quality, presence, and authenticity.

Overcoming the Fear of Change

One subtle barrier to engaging with self-help materials is the fear that change might disrupt the equilibrium of our current life, even if it's an equilibrium dominated by stress.

You might wonder: *"If I start setting boundaries or carving out time for myself, will people think I'm selfish?"* Or maybe you're unsettled by the possibility that newfound calmness could alienate you from your driven, perfectionist social circles.

If your identity has been tied to being the anxious overachiever, who do you become once you're calmer?

Recognizing these fears is crucial. Positive transformation sometimes does threaten old habits or relationships that rely on you remaining "the same."

But stepping into a healthier state doesn't have to burn bridges. Instead, it can open opportunities for more genuine connections.

The people in your life who genuinely love and respect you will likely adapt, celebrate your well-being, or be inspired to pursue their own growth.

And if some don't—if certain relationships hinge on your constant tension or compliance—then reevaluating them might be a necessary step on your path. That can be uncomfortable, but personal evolution often demands a bit of rearrangement.

The payoff is that your new sense of balance and joy can lead you to a life that feels more aligned with your deepest values.

No longer enslaved to others' expectations or the identity of "the stressed one," you might discover aspects of yourself that you'd buried under anxiety.

That discovery is worth any short-lived trepidation about how others may react.

Reading as an Ongoing Process

Think of reading this book not as a linear journey that ends when you flip the final page but as a cycle of growth that you can revisit at different times.

You could skim a chapter that doesn't feel especially relevant right now, only to come back to it a year from now when a new circumstance arises, and suddenly, that chapter glows with relevance.

One advantage of the variety covered in these pages is that it acts like a library of mini-tools and perspectives, ready to be tapped at multiple life stages.

Consider, too, that you might want to read certain sections with a friend, family member, or partner—especially those chapters dealing with relationships, empathy, or boundary-setting.

The synergy of shared reflection can supercharge your transformation.

By reading aloud, discussing exercises, and supporting each other's attempts, you'll find more motivation and glean insights from their experiences, which might differ from yours.

Additionally, don't be afraid to highlight or annotate your book. Scribble thoughts in the margins: "This resonates with the argument I had with John!" or "Try this exercise next weekend."

Those notes become like a personal conversation with the text that evolves as you do.

A Word on Nuances and Challenges

Before we wrap up this *Foreword*, let's openly acknowledge the nuances. Some people might breeze through the breathing techniques and find instant relief; others might wrestle with impatience or self-judgment.

Some might resonate strongly with the journaling prompts; others could see them stilted or contrived initially.

Everyone's emotional wiring is unique, shaped by upbringing, culture, past traumas, or hidden insecurities.

That means the path to "stress less, live more" is anything but one-size-fits-all.

Embracing complexity means allowing yourself to test, tweak, and sometimes discard what doesn't serve you.

If an exercise leaves you tense rather than relaxed, consider adjusting it or exploring a different approach.

If a chapter's perspective doesn't mesh with your worldview, that's okay—take what's helpful and keep moving.

The objective measure of this book's success isn't whether you obey every recommendation but whether you discover new ways to lighten your emotional load and enrich your existence.

Also, mental and emotional states can fluctuate. On days you feel relatively calm, reading about stress management might feel redundant.

On days in crisis, you might suddenly cling to these pages with desperation. That's life, real and unscripted.

Don't be alarmed if your motivation waxes and wanes. You can always return, pivot, or adapt as needed.

Your Role in Shaping the Outcome

Finally, remember that no book, however comprehensive, can single-handedly transform your life without your active participation.

If you're waiting for a miracle to happen simply because you own a copy of "Stress Less, Live More," you might be disappointed. The real magic unfolds when you do the work.

When you experiment with the mini-break adventures, commit to mindful morning rituals or practice setting gentle yet firm boundaries in your personal and professional spheres.

Imagine yourself as a co-creator of this entire endeavor. The authors (and various experts cited or implied) lay out the conceptual scaffolding.

Still, you choose how to assemble, decorate, and inhabit that structure. Your personal insights, comedic stumbles, and triumphant breakthroughs bring these pages to life.

If you feel daunted by the idea of "doing the work," start with a single, teeny-tiny step.

Maybe tomorrow, you set a timer for two minutes of deep breathing. The day after, add a quick gratitude note before bed.

Let these small victories become contagious. No matter how minor, each success affirms that change is possible, gradually leading to more considerable strides.

Foreword Farewell, Book Embrace

And so, dear reader, we come to the end of our *Foreword*.

You've heard the warm invitation, the context, the disclaimers about complexity, and the gentle nudge that this journey demands your active engagement.

I hope you're feeling a pleasant tingle of anticipation, maybe some butterflies in your stomach at the thought of stepping into new emotional territory.

That tingle is a sign you're alive, on the cusp of growth, and about to unravel new possibilities for navigating the world.

Because that's what living more truly entails: noticing the brilliance in small moments, forging richer connections, and trusting that stress doesn't have to overshadow the real treasures of being alive.

Before you turn the page, let me ask one final question: *Are you willing to give this a real shot?* To devote some portion of your mental energy and time, to laugh at yourself when you slip, and to stand in awe when you realize you're growing in ways you never anticipated?

You're all set if your answer is even a tentative yes. Let's do this, step by step, breath by breath, with a light heart and a determined spirit.

Go on, flip the page, and dive into Chapter 1.

The journey awaits. Trust me, it's not only about reducing stress; it's about discovering a reservoir of vitality, creativity, and love that might leave you smiling in the mirror and thinking, *"Wow, I really can stress less and live more."*

CHAPTER 1
FACING THE STRESS MONSTER

INTRODUCTION

Do you remember hearing a sudden clunk in the middle of the night and feeling your heart rate skyrocket, convinced that something—or someone—was lurking in the darkness?

Maybe you immediately flicked on the nearest light and tiptoed through your house, gripping a makeshift "weapon" (a broom? or a shoe?) to protect yourself from the unknown.

There's a good chance you discovered it was just the air conditioner rumbling or your cat knocking something off the kitchen counter. But for a few heart-thumping moments, you were on high alert.

Stress can feel like that: a sudden jolt of adrenaline that leaves you sweaty-palmed and wide-eyed, scanning your surroundings for danger.

Sometimes, the threats are real, but often, they're imaginary. In all their brilliance, our minds can magnify a mundane concern into a towering monster.

Before you know it, you're tossing and turning under your covers at 2:00 a.m., trying to figure out why you can't shake that tension in your chest. Sound familiar?

If you've ever felt your pulse race without an apparent reason or found yourself lying awake wondering what you're doing with your life, you're in good company.

We've all felt that creeping sensation, that little voice that whispers, *"Something's not right. Something's going to go wrong."*

And if you haven't felt it lately, well, you might be one of the fortunate few—so teach the rest of us your secret!

But I'm guessing you're here because you've realized that stress, the uninvited guest at the dinner party, has lingered far too long in your life.

The tension makes your shoulders bunch up to your ears or that constant chatter in your brain you can't seem to silence.

And yes, it can morph into something so big and scary that it feels like an all-powerful monster, overshadowing all the good, fun, or joyful parts of your day.

The problem? Stress isn't some fuzzy teddy bear you can just hug away—it's a complex response with deep roots in our biology, psychology, and environment.

Throughout this chapter, we'll explore three key subchapters that tackle the beast known as stress.

We'll begin by shining a light on *The Realities of Stress*—think of it as pulling back the curtain on everything you thought you knew but never entirely understood about this universal phenomenon.

Then, we'll move on to *Recognizing Your Patterns* because acknowledging your personal triggers and responses will be a game-changer.

Finally, we'll *Set the Stage for Growth*, which means assembling the mental, emotional, and practical tools you'll need to face the Stress Monster with courage—and maybe even turn it into a tiny gremlin that's (almost) cute.

But hold on a second. Let's talk about you for a moment. What made you pick up this book?

Perhaps you're exhausted by the cycle of sleepless nights, racing thoughts, and that relentless sense of being overwhelmed.

Maybe you're a parent juggling endless responsibilities or a student feeling the weight of academic pressure—and the future—bearing down on you.

You could be a professional trying to find some semblance of balance in a fast-paced world. Or you might just be a human being tired of feeling tense.

Whatever your reason, I want you to know that this journey is about giving you a realistic pathway to stress less and live more. After all, we're not robots with an off-switch for anxiety.

We're complex creatures with unique stories, dreams, and heartbreaks. We deserve a roadmap that respects our emotional depth and vulnerability.

Over the following few pages, I invite you to suspend any disbelief about self-help mumbo jumbo. Let's have an honest conversation—one friend to another—about how we can dismantle the Stress Monster from the inside out.

No ridiculous promises, no sugarcoating. We'll keep it real and light, and yes, we'll throw in a good dose of humor.

So, shall we?

1.1 THE REALITIES OF STRESS

Unmasking the Monster

Stress, in many ways, is our body's natural alarm system. It's there to keep us safe from harm. Suppose you ever needed to outrun a hungry lion on the savannah (let's hope not). In that case, you'd be grateful for the adrenaline that prepares your muscles for quick action.

In our modern world, though, hungry lions are (thankfully) rare. Instead, we face looming work deadlines, complicated family dynamics, social media comparisons, and a seemingly endless parade of unexpected bills.

The "danger" we perceive nowadays tends to be psychological or emotional rather than physical.

But here's the kicker: our bodies often respond the same way to a stressful email as they would to an actual predator. Our heart rate spikes, our breathing gets shallow, and our muscles tense up, preparing us for the classic "fight or flight."

That's why your shoulders might be in a constant knot—your body is acting like your inbox is full of lions. Do you ever rub your temples at your desk or clench your jaw during a tense meeting? Yep, that's your primal survival mode in action.

A Dash of Biology and a Pinch of Psychology

A lot going on behind the scenes shapes how we experience stress.

If you love to geek out on the sciencey stuff, here's a little bit of what's happening under your proverbial hood:

- **The HPA Axis**: This stands for the Hypothalamic-Pituitary-Adrenal axis. This phrase describes the chain reaction of your brain and adrenal glands when you encounter perceived threats. Hormones like cortisol surge through your system, keeping you awake, alert, and primed for action.
- **Amygdala Hijack**: The amygdala is the part of your brain that helps process emotions, especially fear. When something triggers it, there is an immediate, overwhelming emotional response out of proportion to the stimulus (directed by the prefrontal cortex). You might freak out over the smallest thing and wonder later, *"Why was I so dramatic about that?"*
- **Feedback Loops**: Stress isn't always a single event. It can spiral. Maybe you feel stressed about your finances, so you lose focus at work. This leads to a lackluster performance review, which increases your financial anxiety, which disrupts your sleep—and on and on it goes.

Understanding these processes isn't just for science class. It matters because sometimes we scold ourselves for *"not being strong enough"* or *"letting stress get the best of us."*

Your body is doing exactly what it's designed to do. Our modern environment often triggers this response more frequently than is helpful, turning our days into a near-constant state of mild alarm.

Stress as the Great Equalizer (Sort Of)

Everyone experiences stress. From the world's top athletes to the humblest among us, no one is immune. However, we don't all experience stress *in the same way.*

Culture, upbringing, personality traits, past traumas, and even genetics can influence how we perceive and manage stress.

Some people thrive under pressure, while others get derailed by a single negative comment.

Take public speaking, for instance. One person sees it as an exhilarating opportunity to share their knowledge (like a rollercoaster thrill).

In contrast, another sees it as the worst exposure (like facing that lion we discussed).

If you're the one who breaks into a cold sweat at the mere thought of speaking in front of others, you might wonder, *"Why can't I be as calm as my friend who practically leaps onto the stage?"*

The answer is partly in your wiring—emotional, psychological, and biological.

This variability means we can't just say, *"Oh, get over it!"* and expect it to work for everyone. Stress solutions need to be as varied and nuanced as stressors themselves.

That's why it's crucial to understand your own version of stress before trying to conquer it.

Stress is not a one-size-fits-all shirt; it's more like a complicated puzzle, each piece shaped by your life story.

What Does "Less Stress" Even Mean?

At this point, you might ask, *"So, am I doomed to feel stressed forever because my brain is wired that way?"* Good question. The short answer is: not necessarily.

The purpose of this book isn't to banish stress from your life like you'd banish an unwanted telemarketer.

Some stress—often called *"eustress"*—can be beneficial, motivating us to meet deadlines, solve problems, and grow. However, we want to address and reduce the chronic, overwhelming, can't-sleep-at-night stress.

When we talk about "less stress," we aim for a healthier relationship with the challenges life inevitably throws us.

We won't transform you into an emotionless android who doesn't care about anything.

Instead, we want to cultivate more resilience—so that when stressful events occur, you have the emotional and mental tools to navigate them without losing your cool (or your sense of humor).

Let's keep going because the next step—*Recognizing Your Patterns*—will give you an even more profound sense of how this stress manifests in *your* daily life and, more importantly, how you can begin to tame it.

1.2 RECOGNIZING YOUR PATTERNS

Spotlight on Your Triggers

Imagine walking into a dimly lit room. You know there's a piece of furniture somewhere—a coffee table, perhaps—but you're not entirely sure where. You inch forward, uncertain.

WHAM! You stub your toe. Only then do you know the exact location of that pesky table.

Stress triggers can be a bit like that hidden coffee table. Sometimes, you only know they're there because you've run smack into them and felt the pain.

Maybe it's deadlines, a particular coworker, or even a specific time of day—like the dreaded 3:00 p.m. slump.

Identifying what sets off your stress response is key.

Without that awareness, you'll keep bruising your proverbial toes on these triggers over and over without understanding why.

So, let's do a quick reflection exercise. Think back to the last week. Can you pinpoint a moment when you felt stressed?

It might have been when your boss unexpectedly asked for a progress report, your child asked you for help with a difficult homework assignment, or even when you scrolled through social media and saw everyone else's shiny, perfect lives (spoiler: they're not that perfect).

Grab a piece of paper or open a note on your phone.

Write down at least three moments you felt stressed and ask yourself:

- **What was happening right before I felt stressed?**
- **How did I physically feel? (Tense shoulders, clenched jaw, upset stomach, etc.)**
- **What was my emotional response? (Anger, fear, overwhelm, etc.)**
- **Is there a pattern among these scenarios?**

This might feel tedious, but mapping out your triggers is crucial.

You might discover that your stress spikes when you have to deal with finances or are pressed for time. Knowing your triggers gives you the power to anticipate them—and prepare.

Identifying the Sneaky Ones

Not all triggers are apparent. Some are subtle, like a gentle drip of a faucet you don't notice until 3:00 a.m., and you can't sleep. You may have taken on too many responsibilities at once.

You don't feel panicked yet because you're convinced you can handle it all.

Then, one minor inconvenience—a spilled cup of coffee or a slow internet connection—sends you over the edge.

You end up feeling bewildered, thinking, *"Why am I so upset over something so minor?"*

The truth is, it's not that single event—your stress cup was already full, and the slow Wi-Fi was the final drop that overflowed.

Recognizing these accumulative triggers requires a bit of detective work.

Sometimes, journaling, talking with a friend, or engaging in a mindful activity (like a quick breathing session) can help you sense the slow buildup before it explodes.

Your Stress Signature

Did you know your body and mind have a "stress signature"? It's a unique combination of physical sensations, emotional reactions, and behavioral patterns that show up when stress takes hold.

Some people get migraines, others get backaches, and still others experience panic attacks or emotional outbursts.

Maybe you get snappy with loved ones, withdraw from social events, or binge on comfort foods.

This is where self-compassion becomes incredibly important.

Instead of labeling your reactions as *"bad"* or *"weak,"* consider them clues. Wouldn't you rather use that information to help you navigate life with more grace?

You're allowed to be human, with all the quirks, sensitivities, and vulnerabilities that come with it.

Breaking the Shame Cycle

Sometimes, stress triggers shame or guilt. We think, *"I should be able to handle this better,"* or *"Everyone else seems to manage. What's wrong with me?"* That line of thinking only compounds the stress.

Before we know it, we're stressed about being stressed. It's like a never-ending loop of self-criticism.

Here's something that might help: Stress doesn't care who you are. It's not about you failing at life; it's about your body and mind responding to perceived threats—real or imagined. And because you're reading this book, you're already showing remarkable self-awareness and motivation. You're *trying*, which is half the battle.

So, let's break that shame cycle right now by acknowledging that stress is universal. You're not alone, and you're certainly not failing.

A Balancing Act

Now, you might be thinking, *"Alright, I get it. I have triggers, I have a stress signature, and I need to be kind to myself. But how does that help me stop feeling so overwhelmed?"* Patience, dear reader.

Recognizing your patterns is the foundation. It's like diagnosing the problem before prescribing the treatment.

You wouldn't expect a doctor to hand you a random pill without understanding your symptoms, right?

Once you see how stress manifests in your life—both the obvious and the sneaky triggers—you can begin to strategize.

That might look like reorganizing your schedule to avoid back-to-back obligations, having honest conversations with people who inadvertently push your buttons, or practicing mini relaxation exercises throughout the day.

The specifics will become more apparent as we continue this journey.

But for now, give yourself a pat on the back for your developing awareness.

You're shining a spotlight on the monster in the room.

And you know what happens when you shine a light on a monster? Often, you discover it's not nearly as scary as you thought.

Next, let's discuss *Setting the Stage for Growth*. After all, awareness is just the beginning. We've got a whole world of options to explore that will help you become a calmer, happier version of yourself.

1.3 SETTING THE STAGE FOR GROWTH

Acknowledging the Hard Truths

The journey to *stress less and live more* won't magically happen overnight. That's not what you wanted to hear, right?

I get it—sometimes we crave a quick fix.

But the truth is that meaningful change takes time, effort, and a lot of courage. I'm not saying that to discourage you. Quite the opposite.

I want to set realistic expectations so you don't beat yourself up if you don't transform into Zen Master 3000 by tomorrow morning.

We live in a society that thrives on instant gratification. Need groceries? Place an online order for same-day delivery. Want entertainment? Stream it, no commercials, no waiting.

However, quick fixes often leave us feeling empty and confused when it comes to mental and emotional well-being.

Real growth is akin to planting a seed in a garden, tending to it daily, and waiting patiently for it to bloom.

Sure, the process can be messy, making you question if anything is growing. But with consistent care, that seed transforms into something beautiful—and so can you.

The Power of Intention

So, where to begin? Let's start with **intention**. What do you really want out of this process?

Perhaps you want to feel a sense of peace when you wake up rather than being jolted by your alarm and instantly worrying about your to-do list.

Maybe you want to show up more patiently for your loved ones or learn to say "no" without feeling like the world will end.

Or you may want to experience genuine joy more often than you currently do.

Here's a small but powerful exercise: write down a sentence that starts with *"I intend to…"* and finishes with what you most desire.

For instance, *"I intend to feel calmer and more confident in my daily life,"* or *"I intend to respond to stress with curiosity instead of fear."*

Don't underestimate the power of simply articulating your goal. When you name it, you can tame it.

Suddenly, it's not just a vague desire; it's a tangible statement you can return to again and again as a guiding star.

Gathering Your Tools

Think about any journey you've taken—climbing a mountain, planning a vacation, or even learning a new hobby like cooking. You need the right tools.

Climbing a mountain without sturdy shoes is a recipe for disaster.

Planning a vacation without a budget or itinerary will leave you stuck in a hotel room with nowhere to go.

Cooking without the proper utensils can turn your kitchen into a chaotic mess.

The same principle applies to personal growth. You'll want to gather practical tools to help you handle stress. These might include:

- **Mindful Breathing Techniques**: Quick exercises to reset your nervous system when tension creeps in.
- **Relaxation Rituals**: A steady routine—like a calming bath, reading before bed, or journaling—that tells your brain it's safe to unwind.
- **Healthy Boundaries**: Learning when to say "no," how to communicate your needs, and how to protect your personal time.
- **Support Systems**: Friends, family, mentors, or even professionals who can provide emotional backing when things get tough.
- **Positive Self-Talk**: An internal script that encourages rather than criticizes. This includes noticing when your thoughts turn negative and gently guiding them elsewhere.

We'll explore these strategies further later in the book, but for now, just know that these tools are out there, waiting for you to pick them up.

And if you ever feel overwhelmed, remember that you don't have to master them all at once. Integrating a tiny slice of mindful breathing into your morning routine can make you more peaceful.

Embracing Uncertainty and Complexity

It wouldn't be fair to pretend this journey is straightforward. Stress can be deeply intertwined with past traumas, ingrained habits, and societal pressures.

You might think you've conquered one layer of stress, only to discover another layer lurking beneath. That's normal.

In fact, it's expected. Sometimes, you'll make progress, and sometimes, you'll fall back into old patterns. That's okay. Think of it like learning to ride a bike.

You might wobble or crash a few times, but each stumble is a lesson in balance. Over time, those lessons accumulate, and you find yourself pedaling with newfound confidence.

Building a New Narrative

Here's something that might blow your mind: You don't have to continue the story you've always told yourself about stress.

If your current narrative sounds like, *"I'm just a naturally anxious person, and I can't help it,"* or *"Life is always out to get me,"* consider how you might rewrite it.

What if you told yourself a story of resilience and growth instead? For instance, *"Yes, I feel anxious sometimes, but I'm learning to manage it,"* or *"Challenges arise, but I'm resourceful enough to handle them one at a time."*

Why does this matter? Because the stories we tell ourselves shape our reality. They influence how we see the world and how we react to it.

Changing that narrative doesn't happen with a snap of your fingers but with consistent reminders and a willingness to challenge negative self-talk.

Think of it like editing a script: you remove the lines that don't serve the plot and add lines that move you closer to your goal.

Mini Moments of Growth

One strategy I love to recommend is "mini moments of growth." Instead of waiting for a big epiphany or a life-altering transformation, celebrate the tiny steps you take each day.

Did you take three deep, conscious breaths before firing an angry email? That's a win.

Did you pause to notice the colors of the sky on your commute home, even when you were feeling tense? Another win.

These mini moments compound over time, slowly rewiring your brain to respond with curiosity and calmness rather than fear and urgency.

The Road Ahead

By now, you might feel a mix of excitement and apprehension.

On one hand, you're ready to tackle this Stress Monster head-on. On the other, you might wonder if you can change old habits. Let me assure you: you are.

And you don't need to become a monk or drastically alter your life to see actual results.

Sometimes, all it takes is being kinder to yourself or setting aside five minutes a day to simply breathe and reconnect with your body.

This subchapter marks the end of our first big look at the stress puzzle. We've peeked at the monster, recognized our unique patterns, and started mapping the path forward.

In the upcoming chapters, we'll explore practical tips, mindset shifts, and daily practices that can help you manage stress.

We'll also discuss boundaries, emotional resilience, healthy routines, and building a strong support system—even if that system is just a small circle of trusted friends or a single confidant.

Let that swirl of emotions be your fuel. After all, growth often begins with the courage to acknowledge both the light and the dark, as well as the confidence and the doubt.

If you're ready, let's keep going.

I promise the best is yet to come.

CLOSING THOUGHTS FOR CHAPTER 1

Congratulations! You've taken a significant step toward living a calmer, more fulfilling life.

It's no small feat to confront stress head-on, and by exploring *The Realities of Stress*, *Recognizing Your Patterns*, and *Setting the Stage for Growth*, you've laid a solid foundation for change.

Pat yourself on the back (seriously, do it!) because self-celebration is an underrated tool in the fight against overwhelm.

Remember, knowledge is only powerful when put into action.

So, here's a quick recap of some practical moves you can make right now:

- **Trigger Tracking**: Write down the top three stress triggers you noticed this week. Keep a log and see if there are common threads.

- **Body Cues**: Pay attention to your stress signature—do you clench your jaw, tense your shoulders, or get fidgety? See if you can catch these cues early.

- **Intention Setting**: Craft that one-sentence intention. "I intend to…" and make it realistic, heartfelt, and positive.

- **Micro-Moments of Calm**: Experiment with a short breathing exercise or a two-minute meditation. Nothing fancy—just close your eyes, inhale slowly, exhale slowly, and observe any immediate changes.

- **Self-Compassion**: When the going gets tough, remind yourself that you're human and that this process is a marathon, not a sprint.

Yes, the Stress Monster can feel big and scary. But every monster shrinks a little when you shine a bright light on it.

You're already doing that by reading this chapter.

Keep that light shining, stay curious, and prepare for the rest of the journey.

In the next few chapters, we'll explore practical stress-busting strategies, from breathing hacks to boundary-setting to mindful living.

You've got this!

CHAPTER 2
MINDSET SHIFT 101

INTRODUCTION

Have you ever wandered through your day feeling like your brain is stuck on a negative track, replaying the same worries over and over again until you're practically convinced the sky is falling?

Maybe you woke up this morning tired, mind spinning with everything you didn't accomplish yesterday, and before you could even take your first sip of coffee, a flood of doubt rushed in.

If you've felt that subtle dread creeping into your mind—like a slow, unstoppable drip from a leaky faucet—then this chapter is your personal invitation to step off the hamster wheel of repetitive stress.

We're about to dive into something I like to call a **"Mindset Shift."** It sounds a bit lofty, and maybe it even feels somewhat abstract. But stick with me.

Whether your worries revolve around job security, relationships, finances, or even that squiggly line on your to-do list that you can't quite decipher anymore, *your mindset is the single most significant factor determining whether you crumble under stress or use it as a stepping stone.*

Think of your mindset like the operating system on your phone or computer—it quietly runs in the background, determining how your programs (i.e., your thoughts, emotions, and behaviors) function.

If your operating system is buggy and outdated, you'll experience crashes, lags, and moments of downright frustration

But update it—expand your perspective, shift your beliefs—and suddenly, you've got a whole new world of possibilities at your fingertips.

Stressful scenarios become less threatening, and life feels more manageable.

This isn't about plastering on a cheesy grin and shouting, "Everything is awesome!" at the top of your lungs whenever you feel overwhelmed. Nor is it about pretending negativity doesn't exist in the world.

We're human, after all. Bad days happen; life can get complicated, messy, and exhausting.

Instead, a proper mindset shift acknowledges the murkiness of reality—both the good and the bad—and finds a balanced path through the chaos.

So, if you're ready, let's break down the walls of self-imposed limitations, adopt a mind that thrives on growth, and learn to see obstacles not as menacing roadblocks but as chances to evolve.

Is that a plan? Great.

Let's jump in.

2.1 BREAKING MENTAL BARRIERS

The Wall We Build

Imagine you're trying to navigate a lush garden full of tall hedges, vibrant flowers, and winding paths. You can smell the fresh scent of roses and hear the gentle buzz of pollinating bees.

But just a few steps in, you see a massive brick wall blocking your view of everything beyond. You suspect there might be more garden on the other side—maybe even a quiet pond or a secret bench—but you can't see it.

Our mental barriers are a lot like that wall. We sense that something good might lurk beyond our line of sight—greater peace, confidence, or freedom from stress—but our limiting beliefs stand in the way.

"I'm not good enough." "I always mess up." "I don't have what it takes." These thoughts become the bricks we stack, one by one, until they tower over our sense of possibility.

If you're reading this and thinking, *"I do say those kinds of things to myself a lot,"* take heart—you're not alone. Most of us experience negative self-talk at some point.

What matters is recognizing that these beliefs aren't absolute truths. They're just stories we've internalized, and any story can be edited, rewritten, or transformed.

Why We Cling to Barriers

You might wonder, *"If these negative beliefs hurt us, why do we cling to them?"* Oddly enough, our brains have good intentions hidden underneath self-sabotage.

Negative beliefs often develop as a form of self-protection. For instance, if you tell yourself, "I'll fail anyway, so why bother trying?" You spare yourself the disappointment (and vulnerability) of putting your heart on the line.

In a twisted way, it can feel safer to remain behind the wall, convinced that you can't climb over, than to attempt the climb and risk a fall. But this "safety" comes at a cost.

You never see what's on the other side of that wall. You never feel the refreshing breeze, watch the koi fish swim lazily in the pond, and never find that perfect spot to sit and reflect.

Fear of failure, fear of success, fear of rejection—these emotional boogeymen trick us into settling for a life of limited growth. The mind whispers, "At least it's comfortable here. Let's not rock the boat."

But deep down, you're probably here because you sense that living in comfort isn't exactly the same as living in fulfillment.

Spotting Your Personal Barriers

Before we talk about breaking barriers, we need to identify them. Let's do a quick exercise:

- **Write down a nagging belief that keeps popping up whenever you feel stress or anxiety.** Maybe it's something like "I never do anything right" or "I'm too old to change careers."

- **Ask yourself: Where does this belief come from?** Did it arise in childhood after a critical parent, teacher, or sibling remark? Did it form in your adult years after a major disappointment?

- **Ask: Is there any actual proof this belief is universally true?** Chances are you'll notice it's more of a perception than a fact. If you believe you "never do anything right," can you think of examples where you handled a situation quite well?
- **Reframe it.** If you believe "I never do anything right," rewrite it as "I'm learning through trial and error, and I sometimes do things right—and sometimes I don't." Notice the shift in perspective from absolute negativity to a more balanced outlook that includes your potential for growth.

This exercise might make you squirm. Confronting uncomfortable truths about ourselves isn't exactly a day at the spa. But it's a decisive first step—like shining a flashlight on the bricks to see how they're stacked.

The Fear Factor

Let's talk about fear. Fear is often the mortar between those bricks, holding everything in place. Fear of the unknown, fear of not being loved, fear of being exposed to who we really are.

Did your heart skip a beat just reading that? It's okay. We all have some hidden or not-so-hidden fears we'd rather not admit.

But here's a little secret: fear is simply a feeling. Feelings aren't facts.

They're more like weather patterns—sometimes intense storms that roll in suddenly and sometimes gentle breezes that barely ruffle the leaves. Weather can change, and so can our feelings.

When you approach fear with curiosity rather than resistance—*"Hmm, I'm feeling anxious about this presentation. I wonder why?"*—you strip it of some of its power.

Suddenly, it's no longer an invisible force controlling you; it's just an emotion you notice, like a passing cloud.

Breaking Through: Courage in Action

Breaking mental barriers doesn't usually happen in one triumphant leap. It's often a gradual chipping away. You may decide to speak up in a meeting when you'd typically stay silent.

Every small act of courage is a hammer against those bricks. Over time, you'll find cracks forming, letting rays of possibility shine through. You'll realize, *"Hey, I didn't collapse in a heap when I tried something new. In fact, I feel kind of proud of myself."*

And yes, you might fail sometimes. But the sting of failure is rarely as devastating as we imagine—and it's almost always accompanied by lessons that help you grow stronger, smarter, and more resilient.

A Practical Tip: The "Stretch Zone"

One practical approach to breaking mental barriers is to operate in what psychologists call the **"stretch zone."** Picture three concentric circles:

- **Comfort Zone**: The place where everything is familiar and safe (but not necessarily fulfilling).
- **Stretch Zone**: The place where you feel challenged and a bit nervous but not completely overwhelmed.
- **Panic Zone**: The place where you're in full-blown terror or overload, unable to think or act effectively.

Aim to spend more of your life in the Stretch Zone. It's where real growth happens: you're pushing boundaries without entirely freaking yourself out.

That could mean volunteering to lead a small project at work, signing up for a new class, or learning a skill that interests you.

Over time, what once felt terrifying might start to feel comfortable, expanding your Comfort Zone and shrinking your Panic Zone.

If you want to systematically approach this, list activities that scare you just a little—not so much that your stomach is in knots, but enough to get butterflies.

Try one new challenge each week or month.

Keep a journal of how it goes.

Celebrate the small wins, learn from the stumbles, and watch those bricks begin to crumble.

2.2 ADOPTING A GROWTH MINDSET

Fixed vs. Growth: A Tale of Two Mindsets

Suppose you've heard the phrase "growth mindset" buzzing around in self-improvement circles.

In that case, you might wonder if it's another trendy term. But it's far from a meaningless buzzword.

The concept was popularized by psychologist Carol Dweck, who observed that people approach life with one of two broad mindsets: **fixed** or **growth.**

- **Fixed Mindset**: Believing your abilities, intelligence, and personal qualities are primarily unchangeable. If you fail a math test, you conclude you're "just bad at math." If you struggle with relationships, you decide you're "destined to be alone." Failure is seen as a dead end, a statement of your shortcomings.

- **Growth Mindset**: Believing your abilities, intelligence, and personal qualities can evolve with effort, persistence, and learning. If you fail a math test, you see it as a challenge to study differently. If your relationships falter, you figure there's more to learn about communication or self-awareness. Failure is viewed as a stepping stone, not a final verdict.

It's easy to see how the growth mindset feels much more liberating. Yet, many of us slip into a fixed mindset without realizing it.

We label ourselves: "I'm unathletic," "I'm bad at technology," "I can't manage stress." Once that label sticks, we sabotage our efforts to grow—because, well, *why try if we already 'know' we can't do it?*

The Beauty of Being an Amateur

Have you ever noticed how children approach new tasks? Hand a kid some crayons, and they'll enthusiastically scribble, unconcerned about making "mistakes." They're not worried about being labeled "bad at drawing." They just draw—and often love every moment of it.

As we grow older, we become *painfully self-conscious*. We want to be good at things immediately, forgetting that the learning process is messy and filled with silly goof-ups.

Adopting a growth mindset means embracing the learner's journey, giving yourself permission to be an amateur, and even messing up in hilariously apparent ways.

It might feel uncomfortable at first. You could see someone else mastering a skill you're struggling with and think, *"I'll never get there."*

But that's precisely the moment to remind yourself: everyone starts somewhere. Even the greatest athletes, artists, and entrepreneurs were once fumbling novices.

Mistakes: Your Unexpected Allies

Adopting a growth mindset can be life-changing if you cringe at the hint of failure. You'll start to see mistakes not as black marks on your permanent record but as data points.

A mistake is simply evidence that something didn't work as expected. Great, now you know! You can adjust your strategy and try again.

When you think about it, mistakes are a form of instant feedback. Imagine you're baking a cake for the first time, and you accidentally double the salt. The cake might taste terrible, but now you know that doubling the salt isn't the right move.

You're equipped with new insight for your next attempt.

Cultivating the "I Can Learn" Mentality

A big part of the growth mindset is the *"I can learn"* mentality. Instead of saying, "I can't handle stress," say, "I can learn how to handle stress better." Instead of saying, "I can't speak in public," say, "I can learn how to speak in public with more confidence."

That simple shift in phrasing is powerful. It keeps the door to possibility open rather than slamming it shut.

Try this:

- **Identify an area where you feel stuck.** It could be time management, conflict resolution, or building healthy habits.
- **Rephrase your goal.** Instead of "I can't do this," try "I'm learning to do this."
- **Create a mini-plan and commit** to a tiny step. For instance, if you're learning to manage stress, you might experiment with a quick five-minute mindfulness session each morning.

Whenever you catch your inner critic saying, *"That's just not who I am,"* counter with, *"But I can learn."*

Over time, you'll watch your mental script evolve from a doom-and-gloom voice to something more encouraging, like a supportive coach whispering in your ear.

Growth in the Face of Stress

We all know stress can feel like a tidal wave, crashing onto the shore of our calm and sweeping us off our feet.

But picture this scenario: a surfer waiting in the ocean for the next wave. Stress is that wave.

A fixed-mindset surfer might think, *"I'm no good at this—just watch me wipe out."* They either avoid the wave altogether, miss the ride, or panic and wipe out early.

A growth mindset surfer sees that wave as an opportunity to practice. Maybe they'll catch the perfect ride or fall, but either way, they learn something.

In life, stress is going to roll in. There's no stopping it. But if you see each stressful event as a chance to refine your coping strategies—rather than as further proof that life is out to get you—then every wave becomes an instructor.

Maybe you'll learn to breathe through an anxiety-provoking situation, ask for help when you're overwhelmed, or reorganize your priorities so you're less frantic.

Each wave, each challenge, is a lesson in disguise.

Practical Growth Mindset Hacks

- **Praise the Process, Not the Result:** When you do something well, celebrate your effort, not just the outcome. This trains your brain to value learning and perseverance over innate ability.

- **Use "Yet":** If you're tempted to say, "I can't do that," add "yet" at the end: "I can't do that *yet*." It's a small word, but it opens a big window of possibility.

- **Embrace Constructive Feedback:** Instead of bristling at criticism, see it as free guidance. It can be tough to swallow sometimes, but it is incredibly valuable if you can hear the lesson beneath the tone.

- **Reflect Regularly:** Keep a journal or simply reflect daily: *"What did I learn today? How did I grow?"* This self-awareness cements a growth mindset.

Adopting a growth mindset takes time. You'll catch yourself slipping back into old, fixed patterns—maybe you'll beat yourself up for failing to meet a goal or for feeling anxious again.

When that happens, pause, breathe, and remind yourself:

"I'm in the process of learning. It's okay to stumble."

2.3 SEEING OBSTACLES AS OPPORTUNITIES

The Universal Truth of Challenges

Here's a reality check: *nobody* sails through life without encountering hurdles. Even the most successful, seemingly confident people have their share of setbacks, heartbreaks, and downright cringe-worthy failures.

Challenges are woven into the fabric of existence—complaining that life is unfair is like complaining that water is wet. It's just part of the deal.

But there's another, often-overlooked truth: these challenges can be catalysts for remarkable personal growth, deeper compassion, and startling innovation.

How many life-altering inventions, social movements, or personal breakthroughs began because someone was frustrated with the status quo?

Pain and inconvenience are a sneaky way of nudging us to develop better solutions.

Transforming the Lens of Perception

When you're in the thick of a problem—say, you're dealing with a job loss, a painful breakup, or a deadline that seems impossible—you might think, *"There's no bright side here. This is just awful."*

It's natural to feel that way, especially if the challenge is fresh. But as time passes and you cultivate a more resilient mindset, you may notice subtle silver linings.

It doesn't mean the situation magically becomes "good"; it just means you're more willing to extract lessons, build new skills, or adapt creatively.

For instance, losing a job might push you to finally explore an entirely different career path you'd daydreamed about for years. A problematic breakup might spark a season of self-discovery, where you learn to stand on your own two feet and develop interests you never had time for before.

It can be hard to see this perspective when you're knee-deep in crisis mode. But keep the possibility in mind: obstacles can, and often do, lead to breakthroughs.

Harvesting the Lessons

No matter how massive or minor an obstacle appears, one of the best ways to transform it into an opportunity is to pause and *harvest the lessons*. This means asking reflective questions like:

- **What is this situation teaching me about my strengths and weaknesses?**
- **How can I do things differently next time?**
- **Do I need to develop any new habits, beliefs, or resources?**
- **Is there an underlying pattern here that keeps reoccurring in my life?**

Let's say you're perpetually stressed by last-minute deadlines. You might discover that you consistently procrastinate out of fear that your work won't be perfect. That's a tremendous insight!

Now, you can address the perfectionism behind your procrastination instead of just forcing yourself to start earlier without knowing *why* you put things off in the first place.

When you take time to harvest lessons, you transform your obstacles into teachers.

Suddenly, challenges aren't just random annoyances sent by a cruel universe—they become turning points that nudge you toward growth and self-improvement.

Reframing: A Mental Makeover

Another strategy for seeing obstacles as opportunities is **reframing**. Reframing means shifting how you interpret a situation, focusing on aspects that are within your control or could be beneficial in the long run.

For example, if you fail an exam, you might initially think, *"I'm a total failure, and I'm never going to succeed."* Reframing could look like this: *"I didn't pass this time, but now I know the format of the exam and the areas where I need more studying. Next time, I'll be better prepared."*

Yes, reframing requires a conscious effort. You have to catch yourself in the spiral of negativity and intentionally pivot.

Over time, though, it can become second nature—your knee-jerk response to setbacks will shift from self-criticism to curiosity and problem-solving.

Balancing Realism and Positivity

Now, you might wonder, *"How can I be realistic about my struggles while also trying to see them as opportunities?"* This is a valid concern.

Going all Pollyanna on your problems might feel disingenuous or even harmful if you ignore genuine difficulties.

The balance lies in **acknowledging the pain while still seeking the gain**. You can admit that a breakup hurts or that a financial crisis is stressful. You can allow yourself to feel sadness, disappointment, or anger.

At the same time, you can hold space for the idea that there's a lesson in it. It's not an either/or situation—it's a **"Yes, and..."** perspective.

- **Yes**, losing that relationship was painful and shocking, **and** it's teaching me to communicate my needs more clearly.
- **Yes**, my business failed, **and** it gave me a crash course in entrepreneurship and resilience.

There's a mature grace in seeing both sides of the coin. It prevents you from wallowing in despair or blindly glossing over genuine problems.

A Quick Experiment: Turn a Complaint into a Possibility

1. **Identify a complaint** you have right now: "My commute is too long," "I never have any free time," "My boss is too demanding," etc.
2. **Reframe it** into a possibility: You can listen to audiobooks or language lessons on a long commute. If you have no free time, maybe it's an invitation to start prioritizing tasks or delegating more. For a demanding boss, perhaps it's a chance to practice assertive communication and boundary-setting.

3. **Take one action** that aligns with this new reframing. Download an audiobook for tomorrow's commute. Reorganize your schedule and see if you can carve out 20 minutes of "me time." Draft an email requesting a clearer timeline from your boss.

Notice if your energy shifts when you do this. Often, you'll feel a little spark of motivation or relief simply because you've redirected your focus from *what's wrong* to *what can be done*.

Building Mental Flexibility

Seeing obstacles as opportunities is a practice in **mental flexibility**. Think of it like doing stretches for your brain.

The more you practice bending your thoughts and perspectives, the less likely you are to snap under pressure.

A flexible mindset can bend in the wind of adversity, while a rigid mindset might break at the slightest gust.

One way to build this flexibility is to regularly put yourself in new or challenging situations—like learning an unfamiliar language, exploring a different culture, or taking up an unusual hobby.

When you challenge your comfort zone in small, manageable ways, you train your brain to adapt, pivot, and remain calm in the face of the unexpected.

Then, when bigger obstacles arise (and trust me, they will), you're more prepared to see them as growth opportunities rather than life-shattering calamities.

Let Curiosity Lead

A curious mind is often a resilient mind. When you encounter a problem, ask questions rather than make statements of doom.

Instead of *"I can't handle this,"* try, *"What options do I have to handle this? Is there someone who can guide me? Is there a resource I haven't yet considered?"*

Curiosity transforms that feeling of being stuck into a proactive quest for answers.

It's like switching from reading a tragedy to reading a mystery. In a tragedy, you assume the story ends badly.

In a mystery, you're motivated to discover *who*, *why*, and *how*—because the end is uncertain, and your detective work matters.

CONCLUSION TO CHAPTER 2

Mindset Shift 101 might sound like a grand promise. Still, it's really about learning how to steer your thoughts away from autopilot so you can chart a new course toward less stress and more fulfillment.

By **Breaking Mental Barriers**, you dismantle the negative beliefs that keep you stuck.

Through **Adopting a Growth Mindset**, you discover the liberating power of seeing yourself (and your capabilities) as flexible, evolving entities.

Finally, by **Seeing Obstacles as Opportunities**, you learn to lean into challenges rather than run from them, harnessing them as catalysts for growth.

None of this requires you to be superhuman or perpetually optimistic. You don't need to grin through the pain or deny the messiness of life.

You *can* still feel your feelings—get frustrated, cry, vent to a friend—while maintaining a broader perspective of possibility.

Stress is real; it's everywhere. But remember, so is your ability to adapt and find solutions.

Each time you practice a mindset shift, you tell yourself, "I'm *not stuck in this stressful pattern. I can learn, evolve, and embrace life's ups and downs with more grace."*

And maybe, just maybe, you'll discover that the Stress Monster we talked about in Chapter 1 isn't quite so frightening when you realize you have the tools—and the mindset—to face it head-on.

Final Thoughts and Next Steps

- **Reflect:** Take a moment (or a journal page) to pinpoint which mental barriers resonate most with you. Are there a few you can actively work to break?
- **Practice Growth:** Pick one area of your life—work, relationships, self-care—and decide how to adopt a more growth-oriented perspective. Maybe it's trying a new approach or asking for constructive feedback.
- **Reframe:** The next time you catch yourself saying, "Ugh, why is this happening to me?" Reframe it: "This is tough—so what can I learn or change here?"
- **Stay Curious:** Put on your detective hat. Stress is an opportunity to explore new coping strategies, not just a reason to feel defeated.

As you close this chapter, consider how these ideas can be woven into your daily routine.

For instance, can you start each morning with a two-minute visualization of a growth mindset?

Can you catch negative self-talk before it spirals, gently swapping it for a more empowering phrase?

The more consistently you practice these mindset shifts, the more natural they'll become.

Chapter 3 will continue our journey by digging deeper into practical methods for dealing with stress, embracing imperfections, and finding healthy, sustainable habits to keep your stress levels in check.

But for now, give yourself a high-five. You've just equipped your mind with a fresh set of perspectives.

Whether you realize it or not, you're already stepping into a new chapter of your life where stress may still pay visits but won't rule your every thought.

Keep going, keep learning, and keep shifting.

Your future self will thank you.

CHAPTER 3
EMBRACING THE IMPERFECTIONS

INTRODUCTION

Picture this scenario for a moment: You're watching a favorite TV show—maybe it's a heartwarming sitcom or a reality cooking competition.

One of the characters (or contestants) spills sauce all over the kitchen floor, ruins the entrée and bursts into a nervous, exasperated laugh.

Surprisingly enough, everyone in the audience finds the moment not just forgivable but oddly endearing.

The spilled sauce, the frantic cleanup, the comedic meltdown—it's real, it's human, and despite the mess, it feels relatable.

Now think about how differently you might have reacted if *you* had been the one with sauce all over your new shoes.

Would you have forgiven yourself so quickly? Or would you have berated yourself for not being more careful?

We often accept flaws in others—especially if they're fictional characters or dear friends—but when it comes to ourselves, it's a totally different story.

We might beat ourselves up for every tiny mistake and expect perfection that not even the best-trained robots could maintain.

The truth is flaws and foibles are woven into the fabric of being human.

They don't define us as failures. In fact, they're what make us enjoyable, lovable, and downright honest.

This chapter is all about **Embracing the Imperfections.**

Sounds beautiful, doesn't it?

Yet it can also feel risky, like venturing into unknown territory armed only with faith that you won't be judged (or that you'll judge yourself less).

We'll explore why flaws make us human, how letting go of perfectionism can set you free, and why finding peace in acceptance is often the missing puzzle in the quest to **stress less and live more.**

Along the way, I'll share relatable anecdotes, thought-provoking exercises, and maybe even a bit of humor—because if you can't laugh at your misadventures, life can get too serious.

So buckle up, grab a cozy beverage (or a spunky playlist if you're more of a music-on-full-blast person), and let's dive into a topic that might change how you see yourself—and the world around you.

3.1 WHY FLAWS MAKE US HUMAN

Celebrating the Quirks and Oddities

Have you ever noticed that the people who stand out in your memory often have peculiar quirks?

Maybe you have a friend who snorts when she laughs or a neighbor who insists on wearing mismatched socks every day.

These idiosyncrasies might initially seem odd, but they're also delightfully human. They break the monotony of cookie-cutter expectations and add color to our interactions.

Imagine if everyone you knew was precisely the same—always calm, always correct, never stumbling over words, never forgetting birthdays. It would be... well, kind of dull.

We often forget to apply that same acceptance to ourselves. Where we'd find someone else's clumsiness adorable, we might label our own as an unforgivable shortcoming. "Oh, I'm such a klutz," we say, rolling our eyes. Yet you wouldn't dream of saying that to your sweet, snort-laughing friend, would you?

The difference is perspective: we give others grace for their flaws but assume our own are fatal flaws. And if we're not careful, this one-sided lens can feed stress, anxiety, and a constant feeling of not measuring up.

We Are the Sum of Our Imperfections (and Our Strengths)

Another way to think about flaws is that they're part of a larger canvas that makes up who we are. You can lose sight of the bigger picture if you zoom in too closely on any single thread—like that minor mistake you made at work or the socially awkward comment you blurted out at a party.

You are far more than a single moment of clumsiness or a one-time slip of the tongue.

Suppose we could see our positive and negative qualities as threads in a beautiful, complex structure.

In that case, we might start to accept that the darker threads contrast the lighter ones, making the entire piece come alive.

So yes, you talk too fast when nervous, but you also have a knack for making people laugh. Or you're terrible at remembering birthdays but the first to rush to a friend's side when they need emotional support.

Those "flaws" might simply be the flipside of your greatest gifts or the little quirks that reveal your personality. Nobody is perfectly symmetrical, and that's something to celebrate.

The Strain of an "Ideal" Self

The idea of an "ideal" self can fuel stress like nothing else. You might have this mental picture of who you *should* be: always graceful under pressure, impeccably organized, and ready with the perfect words in every conversation.

Then you glance at your real-life self—complete with stammering at job interviews, an overflowing inbox, and a pile of laundry you've been promising to tackle for a week—and you feel like you're falling short.

Here's the thing: that "ideal" self is likely a mishmash of cultural expectations, social media illusions, and maybe even parental or societal conditioning you absorbed over the years.

It's not necessarily *your* vision of your best self; it's more like a collage of external benchmarks.

And living under the weight of that collage can be exhausting. No wonder stress creeps in when you constantly try to contort yourself to fit a fictional image.

The Courage to Show Up

If flaws are a natural part of being human, why do we resist them so strongly? Often, fear of rejection or judgment holds us back.

You might think, *"If people see my vulnerability, weaknesses, or past mistakes, they'll turn away."*

Yet, ironically, many of us feel most connected to others when they reveal their soft spots.

Think about when someone admitted they were scared or uncertain; your immediate reaction was empathy.

That makes us human: our capacity to understand and share in each other's fragile moments.

Flaws foster connection. In a world dominated by curated social media feeds and highlight reels, someone who dares to say, "I don't have it all figured out" becomes more relatable, trustworthy, and often likable.

So, if you need a fresh reason to embrace your imperfections, consider that they might be the key to stronger, more authentic relationships.

Reflecting on Your Own Flaws

Before we move on, let's do a quick exercise. Grab a notebook (or open a note on your phone) and jot down a few traits you've labeled "flaws."

Maybe you hate being shy in large groups or blame yourself for being perpetually late. For each one, ask yourself:

- **Is this "flaw" inherently harmful, or have I been conditioned to see it as negative?**
- **How does this trait sometimes help me or others?** (For instance, if you're shy, maybe you're also a great listener.)
- **Would I judge a friend harshly for having this same trait?**

You might find that some "flaws" are pretty neutral or even beneficial in the proper context.

If you discover one that genuinely troubles you—like chronic lateness—then you can approach it as a habit to refine rather than a fatal flaw that defines your worth.

A small perspective shift here can do wonders for self-acceptance and stress relief.

3.2 LETTING GO OF PERFECTIONISM

The Perfectionism Trap

Let's shift gears and talk about a cousin to flaws: the obsession with perfection. Perfectionism might masquerade as a virtue—after all, aiming for excellence sounds admirable.

But there's a massive difference between striving to do your best and demanding perfection in every task.

The former is healthy motivation, but the latter is a recipe for perpetual stress, burnout, and dissatisfaction.

Suppose you've ever spent three hours tweaking the formatting of a single PowerPoint slide or lost sleep over a minor typo in an email. In that case, you know exactly what I'm talking about.

Perfectionism can lead to paralysis because the fear of not getting it *right* can stop you from doing anything.

You might procrastinate on starting a project, ironically, because you dread the possibility of falling short of your sky-high standards.

Why We Chase Perfection

Perfectionism can be rooted in a deep-seated need for control or a desire for approval.

Maybe you grew up in an environment where mistakes were heavily criticized, so now you believe perfection is the only way to earn love or respect.

Or you might see perfection as a shield against judgment—if you produce immaculate work, nobody can criticize you, right? But this is an illusion.

The pursuit of perfection often draws more scrutiny because humans *want* to connect with authenticity. Perfect surfaces feel impenetrable—ironically, they can invite jealousy or suspicion.

The Cost of Trying Too Hard

Let's be honest: trying to keep all those plates spinning without a single wobble is exhausting. Perfectionism can bleed into all areas of life, turning everyday tasks into stress-infused marathons.

You could find yourself re-doing a chore (like rearranging the dishwasher) because someone else's effort didn't meet your impossibly precise standards.

Or you may avoid inviting people for dinner because your living room doesn't look like a spread from an interior design magazine.

Worst of all, perfectionism leaves little room for error, growth, or spontaneity. Mistakes are part of how we learn, innovate, and discover better ways of doing things.

How will you ever create an original masterpiece if you never allow yourself to color outside the lines?

Humor as a Weapon Against Perfectionism

Here's a fun strategy to chip away at perfectionism: *laugh at it*.

Next time you catch yourself spiraling into a hyper-critical state—like meticulously editing a text message for the sixth time—imagine yourself as a comic character.

Perhaps you're a mad scientist in a lab, determined to find the "perfect formula" for a problem that doesn't need that level of scrutiny.

Picture the absurdity of it all. Sometimes humor can give you just enough distance to realize, *"Wait, I'm overdoing it here. This is so unnecessary!"*

When you lighten the mood, you also disrupt the stress cycle. It's much easier to let go of perfectionist tendencies when you acknowledge how downright silly they can look from an outside perspective.

And if you can actually laugh at your mistakes, even better—that's a massive leap toward self-compassion.

Learning to Love "Good Enough"

One of the most empowering realizations is that "good enough" often *is* good enough. That might sound defeatist if you've been indoctrinated with perfectionist ideals, but trust me, there's immense freedom in it.

Consider a small task you do regularly—cooking dinner, for example. If you're a perfectionist, you might insist on following a recipe down to the last milligram, feeling frustrated if you can't find the exact brand of tomato sauce.

But suppose you shift to a "good enough" mindset. In that case, you might improvise with the sauce you *do* have.

Will it win Michelin stars? Probably not. Will it be a tasty, stress-free dinner that nourishes you and maybe even your family? Absolutely.

The same principle applies to work projects, personal goals, and relationships.

Sometimes, letting a project be 90% perfect frees you to spend your leftover energy on something that truly matters.

How to Start Loosening the Grip of Perfectionism

- **Set Realistic Goals:** For each project, define "success" in practical terms. Aim for a specific level of quality and time investment.

- **Use Time Limits:** Sometimes, a firm deadline (even a self-imposed one) prevents endless tinkering. If you say, "I'll spend two hours on this report," you'll work more efficiently and accept minor imperfections.

- **Embrace Small Mistakes:** Allow yourself to make quick decisions. If something isn't perfect, oh well—fix it if it's crucial; otherwise, let it go.

- **Practice Self-Compassion:** Remind yourself that nobody is perfect, and a little imperfection usually makes work feel genuine and human.

Try implementing just one of these steps in your daily routine.

When you see how liberating it is to let go of micro-managing every detail, you might discover that your anxiety lessens and your daily enjoyment grows.

3.3 FINDING PEACE IN ACCEPTANCE

Acceptance Isn't Resignation

Now that we've looked at why flaws make us human and explored the pitfalls of perfectionism, it's time to delve into the heart of this chapter: **acceptance**.

Let's clarify one major misconception: acceptance is *not* the same as giving up. You can accept a situation—or a flaw, or a limitation—and still work toward improvement if that aligns with your values. Acceptance simply means recognizing *what is* right now without pouring energy into denial, shame, or self-condemnation.

Let's say you have a medical condition that requires you to take things slower than you'd like. You might initially resist it, resenting your body for not meeting your expectations.

But fighting reality doesn't make it any less real—it just adds another layer of stress.

Acceptance would look like acknowledging your body's limits and finding ways to work within them or gently pushing them without hating yourself for extra rest.

It's an honest, grounded approach to life that helps you channel your energy more effectively.

A Gentle Path Toward Inner Peace

Think of acceptance as the ultimate act of self-kindness. When you accept your imperfections, you give yourself permission to be a work in progress rather than a final product that must be flawless to be worthy.

That mindset shift can open the floodgates for a calmer, more compassionate inner dialogue. No more raging against yourself for every misstep; no more questioning your value based on a mistake or perceived shortcoming.

If you're still skeptical, consider this. Every moment you spend wishing things were different is a moment you're not spending on personal growth or genuine enjoyment. Accepting reality—both beautiful and messy—frees you to respond with creativity and resilience. It's like clearing debris off a road so you can finally drive forward.

Riding the Waves of Change

Acceptance also comes into play when life hands you curveballs. A job loss, a relationship ending, or a major life transition can all leave you feeling uprooted, scared, and angry.

Initially, it might seem like acceptance would be equivalent to passively saying, "Well, guess that's just my luck." On the contrary, acceptance allows you to anchor yourself in the present moment, acknowledging how things have changed and giving yourself room to adapt.

Think of a surfer on the ocean. If the surfer fights the waves, tries to hold them back, or denies their power, they'll likely be wiped out. If they accept the ocean's might—its ebb and flow—then they can actually ride those waves, harnessing their energy to move forward.

In stressful times, acceptance is like learning to surf the unpredictability of life rather than exhausting yourself by swimming against the current.

The Role of Self-Forgiveness

Often, acceptance is closely tied to self-forgiveness.

You might be holding onto regrets or shame about something in your past—maybe you said something hurtful in a heated moment, took a risk that backfired, or didn't stand up for yourself when you wish you had.

These regrets can linger, morphing into emotional weights that drag you down. Accepting that you made a mistake—truly accepting it—means letting go of the illusion that you can change the past.

It also means recognizing mistakes as stepping stones to wisdom, not definitive proof that you're unworthy.

If you are haunted by a past event, try writing a compassionate letter to yourself. Start with, "I forgive you for…" and detail what happened.

Be sincere about the pain it caused, but also acknowledge the context—your emotional state at the time, the knowledge or options you had available.

Then, conclude with a statement of acceptance: "I accept that this happened, and I release myself from replaying it over and over."

This might feel awkward or emotional, but it can be surprisingly healing.

Practical Exercises to Strengthen Acceptance

- **Mindful Check-In:** Several times a day, pause for a few deep breaths. Notice your bodily sensations, thoughts, and emotions without trying to judge or change them.

Simply observe as though you're a curious onlooker. This practice trains your brain to *see* what is happening without immediately reacting or labeling it good or bad.

- **Focus on the Present**: When you find yourself drifting into "I wish things were different" territory, gently bring your attention back to what you can control right now. Maybe you can improve your situation, or you can't—but you can always choose how to respond now.

- **Affirmations for Acceptance**: It might initially feel cheesy, but affirmations can help rewire your self-talk. Try phrases like, "I accept myself unconditionally right now," or "I am allowed to be both a masterpiece and a work in progress." Write them on sticky notes, put them on your bathroom mirror, or repeat them silently throughout the day.

- **Loving-Kindness Meditation**: In a quiet moment, close your eyes and imagine sending kindness and compassion to yourself, flaws and all. Then expand that circle to include people you love and even people you find challenging. It's a gentle reminder that imperfection is a universal trait, not just your burden.

Embracing Imperfection as a Path to Less Stress

At this point, you might wonder how all this talk about embracing flaws, letting go of perfectionism, and finding acceptance relates to managing stress.

The connection is more direct than you think. Stress frequently arises from resistance—resisting who we are, resisting what's happening in our lives, or resisting the possibility that things might not go as planned. When you drop or reduce that resistance, you free up an enormous amount of mental and emotional energy.

Think of it like this: if you're constantly tense because you're striving to maintain an air of perfection, you'll almost always feel on edge.

Your mind will remain in a state of hypervigilance, scanning for errors and berating you for every perceived flaw. That's exhausting and a guaranteed recipe for chronic stress. But if you allow your imperfections to coexist with your strengths—knowing that being "good enough" is legitimately enough—you remove a tremendous burden from your shoulders.

Similarly, when you accept circumstances you cannot change, you shift your focus from futile resistance to proactive adaptation. Instead of screaming at the sky because it's raining, you learn to carry an umbrella or dance in the puddles.

That mental pivot can lower your stress levels significantly because you're no longer at war with reality. You're working with it.

A Personal Note on Imperfection

Let me share a quick anecdote: I used to triple-check an email for grammatical errors before hitting send. I'd feel my stomach drop if I found even one stray comma after sending it. It was as if a single comma could unravel my entire professional credibility.

The absurdity struck me at some point: I was letting punctuation control my peace of mind. Over time, I decided that hitting "send" with a 95% confidence that it was correct was perfectly acceptable.

Guess what? My work didn't implode, my relationships with colleagues didn't crumble, and I enjoyed my day-to-day tasks more. It was a tiny shift, but it multiplied into far less stress.

I'm not saying grammar is irrelevant or that you should abandon any sense of excellence. But there's a big difference between caring about something and obsessing over it to the point of anxiety.

Excellence can live side-by-side with acceptance of minor mishaps. In fact, excellence thrives when not constantly threatened by an unforgiving internal critic.

Putting It All Together

We've covered a lot of ground in this chapter:
- **Why Flaws Make Us Human**: Those imperfections make each of us unique and relatable.
- **Letting Go of Perfectionism**: Exhaustion, procrastination, and stress often go hand-in-hand with chasing unattainable standards.
- **Finding Peace in Acceptance**: Embracing what *is* in yourself and your circumstances frees you from a perpetual cycle of tension and dissatisfaction.

If there's one takeaway, let it be this: imperfection isn't a problem to solve; it's a reality to honor.

You can still strive for meaningful goals, upgrade your skills, or refine your habits. But do so with a spirit of compassion for your human quirks.

Remember that life is a grand experiment, and part of the fun (yes, fun!) is seeing how you adapt, change, and flourish unexpectedly.

Invitation to Reflect

1. **Identify a situation where you're resisting reality.** It could be a health issue, a less-than-ideal job, or a relationship that isn't perfect. Ask yourself, "What would acceptance look like here? What new options might arise if I stopped resisting and started adapting?"
2. **Examine your perfectionist triggers.** Is it your workspace? Your personal appearance? Your social media image? Write down one specific area where perfectionism drains you, and brainstorm one small action to loosen the grip.
3. **Practice self-forgiveness.** Recall a recent mistake and walk yourself through an honest acceptance of it. Notice how your body and mind feel afterward—lighter, maybe?

Try not to judge how "well" you do these reflections. They aren't tests. They're gentle invitations to look at your life from a perspective of curiosity rather than condemnation.

CONCLUSION TO CHAPTER 3

"Embracing the Imperfections" might be one of the most counterintuitive yet liberating concepts you'll ever adopt.

We're often taught to aim for flawless results in academics, careers, and personal relationships.

Yet flaws are the silent storytellers of our lives, revealing our humanity, forging connections, and teaching us humility.

By letting go of perfectionism and finding peace in acceptance, you're not giving up on growth—you're actually *allowing* genuine growth to happen, free from the shackles of unrealistic standards.

In the quest to **stress less and live more**, imperfection stands as a beacon of hope: an invitation to exhale, cut yourself some slack, and experience life's fullness without the burden of appearing "perfect."

When you let your shoulders drop, your breath flows naturally, and your mind opens to the possibility that you're already enough—flaws, quirks, and all—you might just find that your stress level plummets.

And with that stress dialed down, there's more room for creativity, playfulness, spontaneity, and love.

Keep in mind that embracing imperfection is a journey, not a destination.

You won't flip a mental switch and suddenly feel zero pressure to be perfect.

But each day, you can take a small step toward self-compassion: noticing a critical thought, challenging a perfectionist urge, or simply smiling at yourself in the mirror after a less-than-ideal day.

Over time, these small acts become habits, and those habits become your new normal—a normal where stress has less of a foothold and joy finds a more permanent home.

Now that you've explored the terrain of imperfection get ready to move forward with a lighter heart and a more forgiving mindset.

In the chapters ahead, you'll discover even more practical tools and perspectives to keep shaping a life where you can stress less and live more.

Until then, remember to laugh at your clumsy moments, celebrate your little oddities, and savor the freedom that comes from knowing you don't have to be perfect to be lovable, worthwhile, and genuinely alive.

CHAPTER 4
BREATHE, RELAX, REPEAT

INTRODUCTION

Have you ever caught yourself so lost in stress that you realized you'd been holding your breath? It's a surprisingly common experience.

Sometimes, we worry about What's next on my to-do list? Did I remember to send that email? Why hasn't my friend called me back?—that we forget one of the most essential elements of our survival: **breathing**.

Our lungs don't stop working just because we forget to pay them attention. But the quality of each breath changes when we're tense, upset, or feeling overwhelmed.

We might notice our chest tightening, our shoulders inching toward our ears, and the air barely making it out.

Shallow breathing like that doesn't do us any favors; it can even add to the sense of panic our bodies experience.

That's where this chapter comes in.

We will explore how a simple, natural act—breathing—can be transformed into a powerful tool for calming the mind, releasing tension, and hitting the reset button on your emotional state.

If that sounds a bit too magical, hang in there. While breathing won't solve all of life's problems, it can help us navigate them with **a clearer head** and **a calmer heart**.

But wait—there's more. Once we've laid the groundwork for breathing techniques in *Subchapter 4.1*, we'll move on to *Subchapter 4.2*, where we'll discuss creating a daily relaxation ritual.

Because let's be honest: you can learn all the breathing tricks in the world, but if you don't have a habit or routine that reminds you to pause and practice them, they'll quickly fade into the background.

We'll look at how to weave brief moments of calm into your day—like tiny pockets of peace you can slip into whenever life starts feeling too frantic.

Finally, *Subchapter 4.3* will offer quick tension-release techniques you can use in a pinch—perfect for when you're about to step into a stressful meeting, deal with a chaotic household, or just need a mini reset after scrolling through social media's never-ending doom-and-gloom.

Think of these techniques as your "emergency stress kit," always ready when you need immediate relief.

If you're still skeptical, I understand. It might sound too simple or even cliché. "Breathe in, breathe out," right?

But maybe take a moment to reflect on how often you actually remember to *really* breathe—consciously, deeply, and with intention—on a regular day.

If you're like most people, the answer might be "not often." And that's okay. We're here to change that.

Or at least to help you see how a few deliberate, mindful breaths can act like a gentle hand on your shoulder, reminding you that you can handle this moment—even if your stress is screaming otherwise.

So, before we jump into the details, let's do a tiny experiment together.

Right now, pause for a second wherever you are and take in the deepest, fullest breath you've taken all day.

Inhale for a slow count of four, then exhale for a slow count of four. Did you feel something shift, even slightly? Maybe your shoulders dropped a fraction of an inch, or your jaw loosened.

That's the subtle power of breath awareness—multiply that effect, and you authentically transform your relationship with stress.

You don't need fancy equipment, a yoga mat, or a unique app (though those can be nice extras).

You just need your lungs, a bit of curiosity, and a willingness to try something new.

Let's dive in.

4.1 SIMPLE BREATHING HACKS

Why Breathing Matters

The first question that might pop into your mind is: *"Why focus on breathing so much?"* After all, it's something we do automatically—no instruction manual is necessary.

The answer is that while breathing is an automatic, involuntary process, the *way* we breathe can either heighten or lower our stress levels.

When we're tense or anxious, the body often slips into shallow, rapid breathing that sends distress signals to the brain.

Imagine your heart racing, your chest tightening—your body thinks you're in danger, and it preps you for fight-or-flight.

But here's the good news: breathing is also something we can control—at least in short bursts—by paying attention and making minor adjustments.

Switching from shallow to deep, slow breathing activates the parasympathetic nervous system, often called the "rest and digest" mode.

This process lowers your heart rate, reduces stress hormones, and tells your body (and mind), *"You're safe now. Relax."*

Think about that for a second. With a few intentional breaths, you can literally change your physiological state. That's powerful stuff.

Hack #1: The 4-7-8 Method

One of the most popular breathing exercises is the **4-7-8 Method**, championed by various wellness experts for its calming effects. Here's how it works:

1. **Inhale** through your nose for a count of **4**.
2. **Hold** your breath for a count of **7**.
3. **Exhale** slowly through your mouth for a count of **8**.

Repeat this cycle four times until you notice a shift in your feelings.

Why does it help? The longer exhalation (8 counts) triggers a relaxation response, and the pause (7 counts) enables you to break the cycle of rapid breathing.

It's convenient for those moments when you're feeling anxious or struggling to fall asleep.

If you're new to breathwork, the 7-count hold might feel intense, so you can adjust the numbers slightly. Keep the ratio—exhalation longer than inhalation—to enjoy the calming benefit.

Hack #2: Box Breathing

Another technique widely used—from yogis to Navy SEALs—is **Box Breathing** (sometimes called "Square Breathing"). Imagine drawing a square in your mind:

1. **Inhale** for **4** counts.
2. **Hold** for **4** counts.
3. **Exhale** for **4** counts.
4. **Hold** for **4** counts.

Then repeat. Each side of the "box" is four counts. This creates a rhythmic pattern that soothes the nervous system and helps you stay present.

You can tweak the count—some people prefer 3 or 5—but the uniformity of each phase is what makes it so balancing.

You might visualize a glowing square expanding and contracting with your breath as you do this.

It sounds whimsical, but adding a visual element can focus the mind and amplify the calming effect.

Hack #3: Nasal vs. Mouth Breathing

Have you ever noticed how you breathe when you're rushed or panicked?

Often, we default to mouth breathing—shallow breaths that barely get past our throat.

If you want to encourage more profound, more oxygen-rich breathing, practice inhaling through the nose and exhaling through either the nose or the mouth (depending on the exercise).

Nasal breathing warms, filters, and humidifies the air before it reaches your lungs, which is better for your respiratory system.

It also tends to slow your breathing rate and naturally encourage a more calming rhythm.

The next time you're huffing impatiently through your mouth? Switch to slow nasal breathing.

You might be surprised at how quickly your patience meter starts to refill.

Hack #4: The Sighing Breath

We often associate sighing with frustration or boredom, right? *"Ugh, I can't believe this is happening,"* we sigh.

But there's a positive twist on sighing: a deliberate deep breath followed by a long exhale can release tension.

In fact, physiologically, sighing is your body's way of resetting the breathing pattern. We might inadvertently hold our breath or breathe erratically when stress levels rise. A purposeful sigh can act like a mini reboot button.

Try it: Inhale deeply through your nose, filling your lungs. Then exhale through your mouth with a long, audible sigh, as if you're letting go of something heavy. Do this two or three times.

Notice if you feel a subtle shift in your chest or shoulders like a little unspoken burden evaporates. Sometimes, even the smallest gestures can carry considerable emotional weight.

Making Breathing a Habit

You might wonder, *"How am I supposed to remember all these techniques when stressed?"* Good question. The trick is to weave short breathing moments into your everyday routines. For instance:

- **Morning wake-up**: Before you jump out of bed, take three or four slow, conscious breaths.
- **Pre-meeting pause**: Inhale deeply once or twice before entering a stressful meeting or opening a challenging email.

- **Commute**: If on public transport, practice Box Breathing for one or two cycles instead of scrolling endlessly on your phone.
- **Bedtime wind-down**: Close your eyes and do a few 4-7-8 breaths before trying to sleep.

Small, consistent steps can build a significant shift over time. Think of breathing exercises as seeds you plant throughout the day; eventually, they sprout into a calmer, more centered mindset.

The best part is that they require zero special equipment—just your willingness to pause and pay attention.

4.2 CREATING A DAILY RELAXATION RITUAL

Why Rituals Matter

Picture a cozy, candlelit scene in your mind: soft music playing, the gentle scent of lavender in the air, and a warm cup of herbal tea cradled in your hands. Relaxing, right?

Imagine having a mini version of that serene moment every day—a time you've designated just for unwinding.

That's what a **daily relaxation ritual** can look like. It's a deliberate practice that signals to your brain: *"I'm stepping out of the hustle for a minute to care for myself."*

Rituals matter because they provide consistency in a world that often feels chaotic.

When life throws curveballs left and right, it helps to have an anchor—a small routine you can count on.

It's not about forcing yourself into a strict regimen but creating a gentle framework supporting your well-being.

Designing Your Personalized Sanctuary

You don't need a spa or a meditation room to create a relaxation ritual. All you need is a designated space—maybe a corner of your living room, bedroom, or even a quiet spot at the office.

The key is to imbue that space (or time slot) with intentionality. If you love essential oils, maybe you keep a small diffuser there.If reading poetry calms you, have a favorite book within arm's reach.

Some people find comfort in tiny altars—think of a small shelf with objects that bring peace: a meaningful photograph, a crystal, or a piece of driftwood from your last beach vacation.

Others might prefer a minimalist approach: an empty table and a comfy chair. There's no right or wrong way here. The goal is to make it feel inviting.

Carving Out the Time

Now, here's the tricky part: finding the time. So many of us say, *"I'm too busy"* or *"I'll do it when I have a free weekend."*

But let's be honest—if you wait for a free weekend, you might wait until next year.

Building a relaxation ritual often requires a bit of conscious scheduling. Maybe it's five minutes in the morning before your household wakes up or ten minutes after dinner when you can slip away from the dishes. Could it be your lunch break at work? Or right before bed?

Experiment with different time slots. You don't have to commit to a single schedule forever; find what feels easiest to integrate into your life. The ritual doesn't have to be lengthy—a few minutes can make a difference.

Over time, you might look forward to that daily pause more than your morning coffee or your evening scroll through social media.

Examples of Relaxation Rituals

Not sure where to start? Here are a few ideas. Feel free to mix and match or invent your own:

- **Mindful Tea or Coffee**: Instead of guzzling your beverage while juggling emails, set aside five minutes to sip slowly. Notice the aroma, the warmth of the mug, the flavor on your tongue. This slight shift can turn a routine habit into a mindful moment.

- **Micro-Stretch Session**: A short sequence of simple stretches—like rolling your neck and shoulders or gently bending side to side—can release tension stored in the body. Pair each movement with a deep inhale and exhale for an added dose of calm.

- **Gratitude Writing**: Keep a small notebook. Write down one thing you're grateful for each day. It could be as simple as, *"I'm grateful for my cozy socks,"* or as grand as, *"I'm grateful I found the courage to speak my truth today."* Focusing on gratitude for even a minute can shift your mindset away from stress.

- **Nature Connection**: If you have access to a garden, a balcony, or a park, spend a few minutes outside. Listen to birds, feel the breeze on your skin, or see leaves rustling in the wind. Let nature ground you.

- **Breathing + Visualization**: Combine a simple breathing exercise—like the 4-7-8 Method or Box Breathing—with a short visualization. Picture a calm beach, a peaceful forest, or any setting that brings you joy. This dual approach can deepen your relaxation.

Overcoming Common Roadblocks

Chances are, you'll run into some mental or logistical hurdles. Maybe your inner critic says, *"This is silly,"* or *"You don't have time for this nonsense."*

Remember, these thoughts often echo old habits, especially if you've been running on stress autopilot for a while.

Another common obstacle is guilt. *"I should be doing something productive,"* you might think. But here's a reframe:

Taking a few minutes to restore your mental and emotional energy *is* productive.

It's an investment in your overall well-being, which can pay off by boosting your focus, creativity, and patience.

Remind yourself that self-care isn't selfish—it's essential.

Finally, there's the fear of inconsistency. You might worry about starting a ritual and dropping it a week later.

That could happen; we're all human. The best counter to this fear is flexibility and self-compassion.

If you miss a day, don't beat yourself up—just return to your routine the next day. The point is progress, not perfection.

When a Ritual Becomes a Refuge

Over time, if you stay with your practice—even loosely—you'll notice something magical.

Your ritual becomes like a comforting friend you can turn to whenever stress flares up.

It's not just a chore on your schedule; it's a refuge. A place, a time, or an activity where you can let your guard down and simply *be*.

Think about the effect that could have on your day-to-day life. Instead of feeling like stress is a raging river carrying you downstream, you'll have a calm shore you can step onto whenever you choose.

And that sense of control—of having a safe zone to recharge—can be the difference between feeling overwhelmed and feeling capable of handling life's ups and downs.

4.3 QUICK TENSION RELEASE TECHNIQUES

When Time Is Not on Your Side

Let's face it: sometimes life doesn't allow a ten-minute breather despite our best intentions. Perhaps you're about to step onto a stage for a presentation, handle an emergency phone call, or break up a sibling spat that's rapidly escalating.

In moments like these, you need something fast—techniques that can reduce tension in seconds or minutes.

These quick tension-release methods are like mental first aid—immediate relief for acute stress without requiring a sprawling yoga mat session or a half-hour block of peace.

Think of them as your personal set of panic buttons that, when pressed, help you regain composure and confidence almost instantly.

Technique #1: The One-Minute Body Scan

A full body scan meditation can take 10–15 minutes, but who's got that kind of time in a crisis?

Enter the **One-Minute Body Scan**:

1. **Close your eyes** (if you can) or soften your gaze.
2. **Breathe in** through your nose slowly.
3. In one inhale and exhale, **move your awareness** quickly from the top of your head to your toes, noticing any tension hotspots.
4. **Exhale**, releasing those tension spots as much as possible—like you're letting the stress drain out of you.

You won't catch every muscle group in just one breath cycle, but the mental imagery can prompt your body to release at least some of the tension it holds. If you have more time, do two or three rounds, focusing on a different body section each round.

Technique #2: Progressive Squeeze and Release

When anxious, our muscles often seize up—clenched fists, tight shoulders, or a locked jaw. A quick way to melt some of that rigidity is the **Squeeze and Release** technique:

1. **Pick a muscle group**—like your hands—and **squeeze** for about five seconds.
2. **Suddenly release**, paying close attention to the rush of relaxation that follows.
3. **Move to another area**—like your shoulders or face muscles—and do the same.

Just one or two quick rounds can snap you out of the stress-induced tension spiral, signaling your nervous system that it's okay to relax.

If you're stuck at a desk, you can even discreetly tense and release your glutes, thighs, or calf muscles—nobody will notice, and you'll feel a discreet wave of relief.

Technique #3: The Five Senses Check-In

Sometimes, anxiety or overwhelm hijacks our thoughts and keeps us trapped in mental what-ifs.

One quick way to ground yourself is the **Five Senses Check-In**:

- **Sight**: Name one thing you can see right now that you usually overlook (a subtle color pattern on your desk, a crack in the pavement).
- **Sound**: Notice one sound in your environment (e.g., the hum of a computer, distant chatter).
- **Touch**: Feel one texture (the fabric of your shirt, the cool metal of a doorknob).
- **Taste**: If you're chewing gum or sipping water, focus on the flavor for a moment.
- **Smell**: Inhale and identify a scent around you, even if it's faint.

This process pulls you out of the swirl of anxious thoughts and plants you firmly in the present moment. As simple as it is, it can offer immediate relief from racing worries because your mind can't focus on the what-ifs.

Technique #4: The "I Am Here" Mantra

When stress skyrockets, your thoughts can scatter in every direction—past regrets, future fears, and current pressures.

A quick mantra like **"I am here"** helps you refocus on the now. Say it silently in your mind or whisper it under your breath.

Pair each word with a slow inhale and exhale:

- **I** (inhale)
- **am** (exhale)
- **here** (inhale)

Repeat a few times until you feel more centered. The mantra is a gentle reminder that you're not in the past or future but in this moment, alive and breathing. You can handle *this* moment right now.

Technique #5: The Quick-Release Journal Entry

If you have a minute and something to write (even if it's just a note on your phone), try a **Quick-Release Journal Entry**.

Write down whatever's swirling in your head—no editing, no overthinking, just a raw, free-flowing dump of thoughts. After about 60 seconds, stop.

Read it once, acknowledge it, then close the note or crumple up the paper. It's like transferring the chaos from your mind onto an external medium, giving you distance from those frantic thoughts.

Yes, 60 seconds won't solve a complicated problem. But it can release the immediate mental pressure.

If you have longer, go for it—but even a short burst of writing can be surprisingly cathartic.

Picking the Right Technique

Which quick tension release technique is the best? The one you'll actually use.

Remember that different techniques might serve you better in other contexts—maybe you prefer the One-Minute Body Scan when sitting at your desk and the Squeeze-and-Release technique in a public place with minimal privacy.

The trick is to have at least one or two of these in your back pocket so you're ready when tension strikes. They don't require lengthy training sessions or special gear.

They just need you to pause, even if it's for a handful of heartbeats, and remember that you can regulate your response—if not the situation itself.

CONCLUSION TO CHAPTER 4

Let's take a collective breath, shall we? Inhale deeply and exhale slowly. Feels pretty good, doesn't it?

We began this chapter by acknowledging the simple yet profound power of the breath.

Whether using the 4-7-8 Method, Box Breathing, or a good old-fashioned sigh, these techniques can swiftly transform your inner landscape.

And while learning the exercises is one thing, integrating them into a routine is where the magic happens.

That's why we dedicated a section to creating a daily relaxation ritual—an intentional space in your life that reminds you to pause, breathe, and reconnect with yourself.

It's like giving your mind a mini-vacation daily—no passport required.

Finally, we tackled those moments when life blindsides you with stress, leaving no room for leisurely calming practices.

In those urgent times, quick tension-release techniques become your lifeline: a rapid-fire set of tools to help you ground yourself in the present and stave off emotional overwhelm.

From the One-Minute Body Scan to the Five-Senses Check-in, these methods prove that you don't need half an hour to make a real difference in how you feel. Even a few seconds can do wonders.

You might be thinking, *"This all sounds lovely in theory. Will I actually remember to do it when stress hits?"* That's the million-dollar question. The answer lies in practice and repetition.

You won't always remember—sometimes stress will blow in like a hurricane, and you'll forget every coping mechanism you've ever learned. And that's okay.

This isn't about perfection (as discussed in the previous chapter); it is still about building familiarity with these tools, so they become second nature over time.

Start small. Maybe commit to one deep breath every morning or test Box Breathing whenever you're in line at the store.

Over the next few weeks, try sprinkling these techniques throughout your day as naturally as you might sip water when you're thirsty.

Each time you do, you're reinforcing the message to your brain that you have options—that you're not a helpless passenger on the stress express but a capable, resourceful individual who knows how to slow things down.

And remember, breathing is universal—it transcends age, cultural background, and experience.

From a toddler blowing out birthday candles to an elderly person slowly sipping air through pursed lips, breath is our constant companion through life's joys and challenges.

Embracing it consciously is like inviting an old friend to guide you toward greater calm and clarity.

So, take heart. Suppose you've ever thought you lack the time or energy for stress management.

In that case, these breathing techniques and relaxation rituals might prove you wrong.

You already have what you need—your body, your breath, and your willingness to try it.

Little by little, breath by breath, you can carve out a gentler path for yourself.

You can walk (or run, skip, or glide) through life with a lighter load on your shoulders and a more profound sense of peace in your heart.

Keep these insights close as you turn the page to the next chapter. In the grand stress reduction scheme, breathing might seem almost too simple, but simplicity is its greatest strength.

When we're overwhelmed by life's complexities, going back to the basics—like a mindful inhale and exhale—can be a lifeline, reminding us that we're alive, present, and capable of finding calm, even in the midst of chaos.

And that, dear reader, might just be one of the greatest gifts you can offer yourself.

CHAPTER 5
MINDFUL MOMENTS

INTRODUCTION

Imagine standing in your kitchen, brewing your morning cup of coffee or tea, while a storm of thoughts rages in your head.

Did I send that email? Am I behind on that project? Why did my friend seem distant yesterday?

The steam curling up from your mug barely registers. The comforting smell of your favorite blend goes unnoticed.

Meanwhile, your mind spirals from one worry to another, amplifying the stress of the day before it even starts.

Now, picture an alternative scene: Same kitchen, same beverage.

But this time, as you wait for the water to boil, you take one slow, intentional breath.

You notice the room's warmth, the kettle's gentle hum, and the subtle scents wafting into the air.

You take a moment to savor that first sip—letting the warmth flood your senses—before you even consider picking up your phone or opening your laptop.

Your thoughts about emails or that distant friend still exist, but they're momentarily resting in the background, giving you the space to ground yourself in the present.

That, in a nutshell, is a "mindful moment."

In this chapter, we'll explore what it means to experience *Mindful Moments* in daily life. We'll kick things off by diving into the art of **Observing Thoughts Without Judgment**—a skill many of us desperately need but rarely practice.

Then we'll look into **Cultivating Mindful Habits** because mindful living isn't just about meditating on a cushion; it's about executing small, conscious actions in your everyday routine.

Finally, we'll reveal why **Gratitude as a Game-Changer** can elevate your mood and your entire approach to stress and well-being.

If you're thinking, *"I don't have time for all this 'mindfulness' stuff,"* remember that mindfulness isn't some exotic practice reserved for yogis and monks.

It's an accessible, down-to-earth approach to living that can fit into even the busiest schedule.

And here's the kicker: it doesn't require extra hours in your day—just a shift in perspective.

Instead of drifting through life on autopilot, you learn to notice what's happening here and now.

You become an observer of your own experience, which often leads to a greater sense of calm, clarity, and joy.

Are you ready to gently challenge that restless mind of yours? Let's begin.

5.1 OBSERVING THOUGHTS WITHOUT JUDGMENT

The Endless Stream of Consciousness

Have you ever realized how many thoughts zip through your head daily? According to some estimates, the average person has thousands of thoughts daily.

Admittedly, many of these are fleeting—like random snippets of music or the memory of a dream. But then there are the heavier, stickier thoughts that can loop repeatedly:

I'm not good enough. Did I say something stupid in that conversation? What if I fail at my new project? These thoughts can spike our stress levels and keep us awake at night.

Most of us treat our thoughts like gospel truth, or at least take them at face value. When a negative thought emerges—*I'm so disorganized*—we immediately believe it. Our mind starts listing all the moments we forgot something or messed up a task, reinforcing the belief that we're a hopelessly disorganized individual.

But here's a secret: just because a thought appears in your head doesn't make it true. A thought is simply a mental event, a fleeting ripple in the lake of your mind.

Learning to see your thoughts that way can be liberating beyond measure.

Why We Cling to Certain Thoughts

If thoughts are transient mental events, why do some feel sticky or compelling? The answer often lies in our personal history or emotional triggers.

Maybe you grew up in an environment where criticism was the norm, so you absorbed the notion that you're "not good enough." Or perhaps you once failed a test and latched onto the identity of "I'm terrible at school," which now bleeds into your workplace anxieties.

Over time, these repetitive narratives carve grooves into our psyche, and our brain begins to serve them automatically whenever a related situation arises.

It doesn't help that our survival-oriented brains are wired to look for threats. A negative thought can be seen as a "threat" signal, prompting our minds to keep returning to it in the hopes of avoiding danger.

But in the modern world, that "danger" might be a fear of public speaking or a worry about being left out of social events—hardly life-threatening situations, but our brains may respond as if they are.

Stepping into the Observer Role

So, how do we break free from these unhelpful mental loops?

One powerful technique is to assume the role of an *observer* of your thoughts rather than an *active participant*. Imagine sitting in a peaceful meadow, watching clouds float across the sky.

Each cloud is a thought. You don't cling to the cloud or try to push it away; you simply notice it drifting by. Maybe it's a small, fluffy cloud that says, *"I forgot to text my friend back."* Perhaps it's a massive storm cloud rumbling, *"I'll never be successful."* Either way, it's just a cloud in the sky of your mind.

This approach, often taught in mindfulness practices, can be *surprisingly effective*. Instead of wrestling with each negative or anxious thought—trying to fix it, argue with it, or forcibly banish it—you just observe it. You might label it: "Ah, there's anxiety," or "There's a worry about work."

And then, you let it go—no judgment, no drama.

But Isn't That Avoiding Reality?

You might wonder, *"If I let my thoughts float by, am I ignoring real problems?"* It's a valid concern.

However, observing thoughts without judgment isn't about denying reality; it's about *seeing* reality more clearly.

When you're lost in anxious thoughts, your vision gets clouded by fear or negativity. By stepping into observer mode, you gain a more objective perspective, allowing you to discern which thoughts are worth acting upon and which are just mental noise.

For instance, if the thought *"I forgot to pay my electric bill"* pops up, that's a thought you might want to act on promptly. But if the thought is *"Everyone secretly dislikes me,"* that may be more of an anxious projection than a tangible truth.

By observing that second thought calmly, you might recognize it as part of your fear pattern rather than an actual fact. This clarity can reduce stress and free you to respond to life's challenges more effectively.

Practical Exercise: A Two-Minute Thought Watch

Let's do a little exercise:

1. Find a relatively quiet spot where you can sit for two minutes.
2. Close your eyes or soften your gaze.

3. As thoughts arise—because they certainly will—label them gently as "thoughts." You don't need to describe them in detail or critique them; just silently say "thought" and let them pass.
4. If your mind starts wandering into a story, notice that, too. Then, come back to noticing thoughts as they arise and labeling them.

At first, you might feel a bit silly doing this, or you might find your thoughts racing faster than ever. That's perfectly normal.

The point isn't to stop thinking (an impossible task) but to notice the thinking process.

After the two minutes, reflect: *How did this feel? Did you see any patterns in your thoughts?*

This simple exercise can be a real eye-opener, revealing how frequently thoughts intrude and how we can release them without getting entangled.

Redirecting from Self-Judgment

Of course, the moment you start practicing thought observation, there's a decent chance you'll think, *"I'm terrible at this. I can't stop my thoughts. I must be doing it wrong."*

Let that thought go by as well. Let it be another cloud. You don't need to judge yourself for judging yourself (that can become an endless loop!).

Instead, gently pivot back to a place of non-judgment. Remember: *thoughts happen.* You're not responsible for every weird or negative idea that breezes through your mind.

By observing them and letting them pass, you're taking a huge step toward lowering stress. You're signaling to your brain that you're not enslaved by these fleeting mental events—and that is immensely freeing.

5.2 CULTIVATING MINDFUL HABITS

From Occasional Practice to Everyday Living

It's one thing to have a mindful moment here and there—like a fleeting epiphany during a meditation session or when gazing at a sunset.

But how do we bring that mindful awareness into the daily grind of errands, work deadlines, and family responsibilities?

That's where mindful habits come into play.

If you've ever tried to start a new exercise routine or healthy eating plan, you know that simply having the desire isn't enough.

You need a strategy, consistent practice, and often a few tricks to help you stay on track. The same holds true for mindfulness.

You can learn a breathing exercise or a thought-watching technique. Still, if you don't integrate it into your routine, it'll remain a nice idea you never entirely implement.

The Power of Tiny Habits

A great place to start is by adopting *tiny habits* of mindfulness.

Instead of aiming for a grand 30-minute meditation session each day, which might feel impossible given your schedule, try something more realistic.

For example:

- **One conscious breath** before you open your email in the morning.
- **Three seconds** of scanning your body for tension before you start your car.
- **A quick mental check-in**—"What am I feeling right now?"—each time you sip water.

These small acts might sound inconsequential, but they form neural pathways that reinforce mindful living over time.

Think of them like seeds you plant throughout your day. Eventually, they sprout into a more consistent habit of pausing, observing, and responding rather than reacting.

Habit Stacking

One technique that's been popularized in recent years is ***habit stacking***. The idea is to "stack" a new habit on top of an existing one, making it easier to remember and implement.

For instance, if you already brush your teeth every morning, you could take one mindful breath after you put your toothbrush down.

Or if you always drink a cup of coffee at 3 p.m., you might use the first sip of coffee as a cue to do a brief body scan.

By linking mindfulness to an activity that's already part of your routine, you reduce the mental overhead of remembering to practice it.

Mindful Eating

One of the most accessible ways to cultivate a mindful habit is through *mindful eating*. Chances are, you eat or drink something every day, so it's a perfect opportunity to shift from autopilot to awareness.

Instead of gulping down your food while scrolling on your phone or speeding through a drive-thru, consider these tweaks:

1. **Pause before the first bite**: Take a breath, look at your food, and appreciate the colors, the aroma, or the effort it took to prepare.
2. **Chew slowly and notice textures**: Feel a vegetable's crunch or sauce's creaminess.
3. **Put down your utensil** between bites: This breaks the cycle of shoveling food nonstop.
4. **Listen to your body**: Notice when you start feeling full or satisfied rather than mindlessly clearing your plate.

This simple shift can turn a routine meal into a mini mindfulness session, helping you tune into your senses, hunger cues, and emotions surrounding food.

As you become more conscious of what your body actually needs, it can also reduce stress-related eating or overeating.

Mindfulness in Motion

You don't have to be still and silent to practice mindfulness.

Activities like walking, running, or even doing household chores can become mindful when you tune into the present moment.

For example, if you're folding laundry, feel the texture of the fabric, notice the colors, and pay attention to the repetitive motion of folding. If your mind wanders, *"I can't believe I'm stuck doing this again. I have so much else to do!"*—acknowledge that thought and gently return your focus to the physical sensation of the chore.

The same goes for walking. Instead of racing to your destination with your mind on your next task, slow down and notice the placement of each foot on the ground. Feel the breeze on your skin. Notice the shapes of clouds overhead or the sounds of traffic humming in the distance.

Again, if your thoughts drift, that's okay—just bring them back to the sensory details of the walk.

This mindful walking can transform a mundane errand into a grounding, rejuvenating experience.

Tech-Assisted Mindfulness

Let's face it: technology is deeply woven into our lives and can distract and assist us. Rather than fighting it, consider using technology to support mindful habits.

Apps that remind you to breathe or pause can be surprisingly helpful. Some apps offer quick guided meditations or check-ins, allowing you to incorporate mindfulness during short breaks throughout the day.

However, it's crucial to maintain balance. If you find yourself mindlessly scrolling through a mindfulness app (yes, that can happen!), it might be a sign to step away from the screen and practice a simple, self-guided technique instead.

Technology should be a tool, not a trap.

Overcoming Resistance

Chances are, you'll hit moments of resistance. You might think, *"I'm too busy,"* or *"This feels forced,"* or *"I'm not in the mood to be mindful right now."* That's normal.

Mindfulness asks us to step out of our mental chatter and autopilot habits, which can feel uncomfortable at first—especially if we're accustomed to constant stimulation or distraction.

This discomfort is a sign that you're stretching beyond your comfort zone. Acknowledge it, welcome it as part of the process, and gently continue.

One helpful approach is to get curious about your resistance.

If you find yourself avoiding mindfulness, ask, *"What am I worried I'll find if I actually slow down and pay attention?"*

Sometimes, it's a buried anxiety or a fear of confronting difficult emotions. Ironically, pushing those emotions away tends to feed stress in the long run, whereas facing them mindfully can dissipate their hold on you.

The Payoff

Life gains a richer texture when mindfulness becomes woven into your daily habits.

You may start to notice small joys you used to overlook: the way sunlight filters through your window in the morning, the comforting sound of rain, the kindness of a stranger holding a door open.

Stressful events might still happen—of course, they will—but your response shifts.

Instead of being swept away in a torrent of reactivity, you develop a capacity to pause, breathe, and choose a more grounded reply. And that shift can transform the entire rhythm of your life, allowing you to stress less and genuinely live more.

5.3: GRATITUDE AS A GAME-CHANGER

Beyond the Buzzword

Gratitude is a concept that gets tossed around often, from motivational posters to social media hashtags. Yet, it can also feel hollow if we don't engage with it sincerely.

"Just be grateful!" people say, as though it's a magic wand that instantly eradicates all troubles.

But like mindfulness, gratitude isn't a quick fix; it's a practice that, when approached thoughtfully, has the power to shift your perspective in profound ways.

Why Gratitude Works

Have you ever noticed that your mind tends to stick to negative events more than positive ones? That's your survival brain doing its job.

Our ancestors needed to focus on threats (like predators or food shortages) to stay alive.

This negativity bias is still kicking around in our modern minds, which explains why a single piece of negative feedback can overshadow a hundred compliments.

Gratitude acts as a gentle counterbalance to this bias. By focusing on what we appreciate—rather than what we fear or resent—we train our brains to notice life's gifts more readily.

Research has shown that consistent gratitude practice can improve sleep, enhance relationships, and boost immune function.

That's right: counting your blessings might be one of the most low-effort, high-impact stress busters.

Real Gratitude vs. Forced Positivity

Let's be clear: practicing gratitude doesn't mean you plaster a fake smile and pretend everything's sunshine and rainbows.

Life can be challenging, and acknowledging difficulties is crucial for emotional health.

Genuine gratitude is about recognizing good things amidst challenges.

It might look like saying, "I'm really struggling with my job right now, but I do appreciate that my co-worker took time to help me on a project," or "I'm frustrated about this unexpected bill, but I'm thankful I have a roof over my head tonight."

This nuance matters. Forced positivity—where you insist you *must* feel grateful for everything all the time—can backfire, leading to denial of genuine feelings.

Authentic gratitude allows space for complexity, acknowledging that life isn't perfect but still contains moments of beauty, kindness, or simple comfort.

Building a Gratitude Practice

If you'd like to make gratitude a daily habit, here are a few suggestions:

- **Gratitude Journal**: Set aside a few minutes at the end of each day to write down three things you're grateful for. They can be significant (like a loved one recovering from an illness) or small (like a tasty cookie you enjoyed). The key is consistency—do it every day, even if you're tired or cranky.

- **Thank-You Notes or Messages**: Sending a short message of thanks to someone—a family member, friend, or even a service provider—can deepen your gratitude and brighten someone else's day. It's a two-for-one deal in the positivity department.

- **Gratitude Trigger**: Pick a daily routine—like locking your door when leaving the house—and use it as a cue to think of one thing you're grateful for. If you do this consistently, you'll start associating that action with gratitude, creating a powerful mental link.

- **Verbal Expression**: Whenever you notice something you appreciate—a beautiful sunset, a thoughtful gesture—say it out loud. Even if you're alone, giving voice to your thanks can reinforce the feeling.

The Emotional Impact

Over time, a steady gratitude practice can reshape the emotional landscape of your life. You may become more resilient to setbacks.

You'll still feel disappointed when something goes wrong—like a missed promotion or a delayed flight.

Still, you'll also have a habit of spotting silver linings or other remaining blessings.

This doesn't mean you won't ever feel stress or sadness; it simply means that those feelings won't be your only reality.

Gratitude also fosters connection. When you consistently acknowledge the good in others, you nurture more profound, more empathetic relationships.

People respond to genuine appreciation. If you start thanking your partner for small acts of kindness—like making your coffee or taking out the trash—you may see a surge in warmth and goodwill at home.

It's not about manipulation; it's about mutual respect and noticing each other's efforts in a world that often overlooks them.

Gratitude in Tough Times

But what about genuinely hard times, like losing a job, facing health issues, or enduring the breakdown of a relationship?

That's where gratitude becomes both more challenging and more crucial.

Finding even the tiniest thread of appreciation amid hardship can keep you from drowning in despair.

It might be as minimal as being grateful for having a supportive friend or being thankful for the courage to face another day, even if you feel broken inside.

This isn't about trivializing pain or glossing over life's rough patches. It's about sustaining a lifeline of hope and perspective.

Sometimes, that tiny spark of gratitude helps us see a path forward, reminding us that not all is lost and that better days might still lie ahead.

Combining Mindfulness and Gratitude

Mindfulness and gratitude complement each other beautifully.

When you're mindful, you notice the details of your surroundings and experiences, which naturally leads to an appreciation for what you observe—like the texture of a tree's bark, the laughter of a child, or the taste of a home-cooked meal.

Conversely, when you're feeling grateful, it's easier to stay present because your mind is focused on what's here and now rather than what's lacking.

Try weaving these two practices together. For instance, take a mindful walk and look for things you appreciate—colors, shapes, sounds, or memories the walk evokes.

Or merge gratitude with a mindful eating practice, savoring each bite and feeling thankful for the nourishment it provides.

The interplay between mindfulness and gratitude can be like adding flavor to a dish—it enlivens the entire experience, making it richer and more fulfilling.

CONCLUSION TO CHAPTER 5

We began this chapter by considering the power of **Mindful Moments**. Whether sipping your morning coffee or strolling in your neighborhood, the simplest activities can become opportunities for profound awareness.

We explored **Observing Thoughts Without Judgment**, discovering that not every thought deserves our unwavering attention or belief.

By stepping into the role of an observer, you free yourself from the grip of negative rumination and open up mental space for creativity, calm, and clear-headed decision-making.

Then, we delved into **Cultivating Mindful Habits**—the practical how-to of living mindfully in a world that's anything but.

From tiny habits like taking one conscious breath before checking emails to more structured practices like mindful eating, these small shifts in behavior accumulate over time, steering your life toward a more centered and less stressed existence.

Even everyday chores can become mini-meditations if you approach them with presence and a willingness to observe your thoughts and emotions.

Finally, **Gratitude as a Game-Changer**—not as a glib positivity tool, but as a genuine practice that balances our inborn negativity bias and sheds light on the overlooked blessings around us.

By consistently focusing on what we appreciate—amid life's challenges, chaos, and unpredictability—we cultivate resilience, deepen relationships, and foster an internal environment better equipped to handle stress.

So, where do you go from here? You might start with just one mindful breath tomorrow morning or end your day by writing down something you're grateful for.

You might catch yourself spiraling into negative self-talk and instead pause to observe your thoughts without judging them.

Any one of these simple, seemingly small choices can plant the seeds of a more mindful, gratitude-filled life.

Over time, these seeds blossom into a robust practice that cushions you against the stressors you face each day—transforming the ordinary into something just a bit more extraordinary.

Remember, this is a journey of exploration, not a race to perfection. You will sometimes slip back into autopilot, and you may forget to keep that gratitude journal or drop your mindful habits for a week when life gets hectic.

That's okay.

Each moment, each breath is a chance to begin anew. Whether you're a mindfulness novice or a seasoned practitioner, there's always another layer of awareness to uncover, another shade of gratitude to experience.

And that makes the journey worth taking—an ongoing discovery of how to **stress less** and **live more**, one mindful moment at a time.

CHAPTER 6
MASTERING EMOTIONAL WAVES

INTRODUCTION

Picture the ocean for a moment: vast, mysterious, and ever-changing.

Some days, it's tranquil—clear waters gently lapping at the shore under a warm sun.

Other days, it's choppy, filled with crashing waves that threaten to knock you off your feet if you step too close.

Now, think about your emotional life in the same way. Isn't it a lot like an ocean, with highs and lows that can feel peaceful one minute and completely overwhelming the next?

We've all had those moments when a sudden swell of emotion crashes over us—maybe it's anger flaring because someone cut us off in traffic or anxiety creeping in when we wake up at 3 a.m. with a racing mind.

Or perhaps you've experienced the opposite: a wave of unexpected joy that warms your heart and reminds you that life can be brighter than you thought just a few hours earlier.

Emotions, like waves, have their own rhythm. The good news? You can learn to ride them without getting fully submerged.

In this chapter, we're diving deep into the art of **Mastering Emotional Waves**.

We'll start with **Identifying Emotional Triggers** (Subchapter 6.1) to understand why certain situations or people can set us off so intensely.

Then, we'll move on to **Riding the Ups and Downs** (Subchapter 6.2), exploring how to navigate the inevitable fluctuations in our emotional weather.

Finally, we'll look at **Emotional Resilience Tactics** (Subchapter 6.3), practical tools, and strategies to help you bounce back when life's storms hit.

As you read through, I encourage you to imagine each emotional surge in your life as a wave forming on the horizon.

Sometimes, it looks ominous; other times, it's surprisingly beautiful. But just as surfers learn to keep their balance and adapt to each wave, you can learn to do the same with your emotions.

No, it's not about suppressing your feelings or pretending your challenges don't exist.

It's about acknowledging the power of your internal ocean, respecting its currents, and cultivating the skill to swim (or surf!) with confidence.

By the end of this chapter, I hope you'll feel more equipped to stay afloat—even when the waters get rough.

6.1 IDENTIFYING EMOTIONAL TRIGGERS

The Hidden Switches That Set Us Off

We've all been there: a conversation takes a sudden turn, and before you know it, you're fuming or on the verge of tears. A single comment from a colleague brings up old insecurities, or your significant other forgets a small detail, and you find yourself inexplicably upset.

These reactions don't spring from thin air; they're often linked to emotional triggers—those hidden "switches" that, once flipped, release a flood of feelings.

An emotional trigger can be anything: a word, a tone of voice, a memory, a person, a setting, or even a particular smell.

They're rooted in past experiences—both good and bad. For instance, if you once had a teacher who publicly embarrassed you for making a mistake, you might find yourself reacting disproportionately to any criticism at work, even constructive criticism.

Or suppose a particular song was playing during a tough breakup. In that case, you might instantly feel anxious or sad whenever it comes on the radio.

Why Triggers Matter

Identifying emotional triggers is essential for several reasons. First, it helps you understand that your intense reactions aren't random or "crazy."

They're your mind's way of trying to protect you from perceived danger, shaped by past hurts or fears.

Second, once you know what triggers you, you can develop strategies to cope more effectively.

Instead of being blindsided by a wave of emotion, you see it forming in the distance and can prepare yourself.

Think of your triggers as personalized "warning signs" along a road.

The signs aren't there to shame or suggest you're weak; they're there to inform you.

If you ignore them, you risk careening off an emotional cliff. If you heed them, you can slow down, shift gears, and steer your reaction in a healthier direction.

Taking an Emotional Inventory

If you're unsure of what sets you off, consider doing a brief emotional inventory:

- **Reflect on recent emotional spikes**: Jot down the last few times you felt a sudden rush of anger, sadness, fear, or any other intense emotion.
- **Identify commonalities**: Ask yourself what was happening in those moments. Who was there? What was being discussed? Were any specific words, sounds, or actions preceding your reaction?
- **Explore your backstory**: Can you trace this trigger to an earlier life event or recurring pattern? Maybe you realize you always get anxious around people who remind you of a critical family member, or you feel defensive when someone questions your competence because you once struggled in school.

This process can be surprisingly enlightening. Sometimes, just naming a trigger can reduce its power because you're no longer in the dark about why you feel the way you do.

Triggers vs. Boundaries

It's crucial to differentiate between emotional triggers and legitimate boundaries.

A boundary might be something like "I won't let someone yell at me or call me names," which is a healthy standard for respectful interaction.

On the other hand, a trigger might be feeling panic when anyone raises their voice slightly—*even if* they're not yelling at you but are just excited or upset about something else.

Recognizing this difference can help you communicate effectively. You can calmly say, "Hey, when voices get loud, I feel anxious because of past experiences. Could we lower our voices and talk this through?"

That way, you honor your emotional reality without blaming the other person for something they may not even realize they're doing.

The Role of Belief Systems

Another aspect to consider is how your belief systems shape your triggers.

If you believe, for instance, that making mistakes is a sign of failure, you may find it extremely triggering whenever someone points out an error.

If you think you're responsible for everyone else's happiness, you'll feel panic whenever conflict arises.

By questioning these underlying beliefs—*Is this really true? Does one mistake define me? Am I responsible for everyone's mood?*—you can start dismantling triggers at their root.

Practical Exercise: Trigger Tracking

Try keeping a "Trigger Tracking" log for a week:

- **Event/Context**: Where were you? What happened?
- **Emotion**: What did you feel—anger, shame, hurt, fear, or something else?
- **Intensity**: Rate the intensity from 1 (mild) to 10 (overwhelming).
- **Possible Trigger**: What might have set you off?
- **Past Connection**: Does this remind you of a past situation or worry?
- **Constructive Response**: How could you handle it differently next time?

Reviewing this log can reveal patterns you never realized were there—like how certain times of the day or stress levels make you more susceptible to triggers.

Or maybe you'll find that a specific type of comment (e.g., about your appearance or work ethic) repeatedly leads to hurt feelings.

Once these patterns become apparent, you're better positioned to manage them.

Gentle Self-Compassion

Be kind to yourself as you uncover triggers; triggers often form around unresolved wounds.

Instead of judging yourself—*"Ugh, I'm so sensitive!"*—acknowledge that your emotional system is doing its best to protect you.

Embracing a compassionate stance helps you approach triggers with curiosity rather than shame.

You might say, *"Okay, I see that I got really upset when I felt excluded. I wonder if this traces back to some old insecurity? Let's explore that."*

That shift in attitude can soften the impact of the wave before it even crashes.

Identifying emotional triggers is the crucial first step in mastering your emotional waves.

Once you know what sets you off, you can take proactive steps in the next phase: learning to ride those ups and downs without losing yourself in the swell.

6.2 RIDING THE UPS AND DOWNS

Emotions as Waves, Not Permanent States

Imagine you're at the beach, standing knee-deep in water. A wave approaches—sometimes, it's small and barely makes you wobble; other times, it's a chest-high swell that threatens to knock you over.

Yet, no matter how big or forceful, each wave eventually recedes. Emotions work the same way.

They surge, build to a peak, and then subside, even if it doesn't feel like it in the heat of the moment.

One of the biggest illusions about emotions is the fear that a certain feeling—be it sadness, anger, or anxiety—will last forever.

This fear can make an already uncomfortable emotion feel utterly catastrophic.

But here's the truth: no emotion is permanent. Recognizing the transient nature of feelings can provide immense relief.

It's like telling yourself, *"I may be feeling anxious now, but this wave will pass eventually."*

Observing the Emotional Wave

To ride an emotional wave effectively, start by observing it. This might sound abstract, but it's a practical skill.

Next time you feel an emotional surge, pause for a moment if you can:

1. **Name the emotion**: "Okay, I'm feeling anger right now."
2. **Notice the physical sensations**: Is your jaw clenched, heart racing, stomach tight? Do you feel the heat rising to your face?
3. **Assess intensity**: On a scale of 1 to 10, how strong is this emotion?
4. **Recognize the urge**: When we're swept up in emotion, we often have a corresponding urge—to yell, to run away, to isolate, to seek reassurance. Observe that urge without immediately acting on it.

Doing this creates a moment of mindfulness—a small gap between the emotion and your reaction. That gap is where choice lives.

Instead of being at the mercy of the wave, you learn to surf it, maintaining some balance as it swells beneath you.

The Power of "Surfing" Discomfort

"Surfing" is a term many therapists use to describe riding out uncomfortable emotions.

Just as a surfer balances on a surfboard, adjusting their posture to flow with the changing contours of the wave, you learn to stay present with your feelings rather than fighting them.

Fighting an emotion often intensifies it—like thrashing in the water, which can increase your risk of drowning.

But if you allow the emotion to rise and fall, you're more likely to remain stable until it passes.

This doesn't mean you have to love or enjoy the feeling. It's natural to wish those emotions would vanish if you're angry or deeply sad.

Surfing simply means acknowledging, *"This is what I'm feeling right now,"* and choosing not to escalate the feeling by adding extra mental commentary—like catastrophizing or self-blame.

Your breath can be an anchor here: focusing on slow, deep inhalations and exhalations helps you stay grounded when the emotional wave feels massive.

Finding Constructive Outlets

Riding emotional waves also involves channeling them in a healthy direction, especially when the emotion is intense.

For instance, if you're seething with anger, stuffing it down isn't the answer—but neither is unleashing it on an innocent bystander.

You might find a middle path by expressing your anger in a contained way: writing in a journal, talking it out with a trusted friend or therapist, or even engaging in physical activity to release pent-up energy.

Similarly, if sadness or anxiety floods you, consider simple, grounding activities.Some people find solace in walking, doing light stretches, or playing calming music. Others benefit from creative pursuits like drawing or playing an instrument.

The goal is to acknowledge the emotion and give it space to move through you rather than letting it fester or erupt in destructive behavior.

Balancing Positive and Negative Emotions

We often talk about negative emotions as waves to be ridden.

Still, positive emotions can come in waves, too—like excitement, delight, or a burst of motivation.

Riding positive waves is about savoring those moments without clinging to them. Clinging can backfire; if you try desperately to hold onto a joyful feeling, fear of losing it can creep in.

Instead, enjoy it fully while it's there, grateful that life has these unexpected gifts.

When it ebbs, as it will, practice letting go gracefully, knowing that more positive waves will come around in time.

Emotional Hangovers

After an intense emotional wave—especially a negative one—you might experience an "emotional hangover."

This is the aftermath where you feel drained, foggy, or regretful about anything you said or did in the heat of the moment. It's essential to practice self-forgiveness here.

Beating yourself up only prolongs the negative cycle. A healthier approach is to reflect constructively: *"What triggered me? How could I handle it differently next time?"*

Then offer yourself kindness—because growing emotional mastery is a lifelong process, and slip-ups are bound to happen.

When to Seek Help

While most emotional waves can be surfed with mindful awareness and self-care strategies, sometimes the waves come in tsunamis.

If you find yourself regularly overwhelmed by extreme moods, or if your emotional states interfere with daily functioning or lead to harmful behaviors, it might be time to seek professional help.

Therapists, counselors, and support groups can offer tailored techniques and empathetic listening that accelerate your ability to manage intense emotions safely.

Riding the ups and downs is an ongoing dance with your emotional nature.

It's about acknowledging that you can't control every wave that comes your way, but you *can* control how you respond.

And as with any dance or sport, practice is key. The more you gently allow yourself to feel without judgment, the quicker you'll find your footing in turbulent waters.

Once you've got the basics of navigating emotional peaks and troughs, you'll be well-prepared to explore the final part of this chapter: building long-lasting emotional resilience.

6.3: EMOTIONAL RESILIENCE TACTICS

What Is Emotional Resilience?

If riding emotional waves is about moment-to-moment coping, emotional resilience is the broader capacity that keeps you afloat through life's storms.

It's the "bounce-back" quality—your ability to recover from setbacks, adapt to change, and keep going in the face of adversity.

Resilience doesn't mean you never feel pain or sadness; it means you have the inner resources to heal, learn, and grow from difficult experiences.

Think of resilience as a muscle you can strengthen. Some people seem born with naturally high resilience, thanks to genetics or supportive early environments.

However, anyone can develop it further. And just like physical training, emotional resilience improves when we engage in regular, purposeful practice.

Tactic #1: Self-Compassion

When life knocks you down, how do you talk to yourself? Do you berate yourself for being "weak" or "incapable," or do you offer the same kindness you would to a dear friend?

Self-compassion is an essential resilience-building tactic because it turns off the harsh inner critic and replaces it with a nurturing inner coach.

- **Acknowledge the struggle**: "This is really hard right now. I'm feeling overwhelmed."
- **Recognize common humanity**: "I'm not alone in feeling this way; many people face similar challenges."

- **Practice gentle self-talk**: "I can take things one step at a time. I deserve support and kindness, just like anyone else."

This mindset doesn't magically solve your problems, but it creates an emotional environment where healing and problem-solving are more likely to happen. Instead of pouring salt on your wounds, you offer them soothing balm.

Tactic #2: Healthy Routines

Resilience often flourishes in the soil of stable, healthy routines. Even small emotional waves can feel overwhelming when you're physically run-down, disorganized, or lacking social support.

Consider these routine-related elements:

- **Sleep**: Aim for consistent, restful sleep. Chronic sleep deprivation can amplify negative emotions and reduce your emotional control.
- **Nutrition**: Balanced meals and staying hydrated are surprisingly crucial for mood regulation.
- **Exercise**: Regular movement—whether it's walking, yoga, or hitting the gym—helps burn off stress hormones and boost endorphins.
- **Social Connections**: A supportive network of friends or family can act as a buffer against stress, offering perspective and empathy.

These basics might sound obvious, but they're the foundation for emotional resilience.

If your daily life is chaotic—skipping meals, sleeping four hours a night, isolating yourself socially—your capacity to handle emotional storms diminishes.

Tidy up your routines first, and you'll notice an immediate uplift in your emotional strength.

Tactic #3: Cognitive Flexibility

Resilient people often display what psychologists call "cognitive flexibility": the ability to see problems or challenges from multiple angles and adapt their thinking as needed.

They don't get stuck in a mental rut if something doesn't go as planned.

They experiment with solutions, consider new perspectives, or pivot their approach entirely.

For instance, if you lose a job, a non-resilient mindset might say, *"This is a disaster. I'm unemployable. My life is over."*

A resilient mindset might acknowledge the disappointment and ask, *"Okay, what can I learn from this? Could this be an opportunity to try a different career path or upgrade my skills?"*

Reframing the situation will lessen the emotional blow and open the door to creative problem-solving.

Tactic #4: Meaning and Purpose

Another cornerstone of resilience is having a sense of meaning or purpose.

This doesn't necessarily mean finding your "one true calling" in life.

It could be anything from caring for your family to advocating for a cause you believe in, from pouring yourself into artistic endeavors to volunteering in your community.

When you connect with something bigger than yourself, you gain a reason to keep going, even when emotional waves threaten to pull you under.

Ask yourself, *"What do I value most?"* and *"How can I align my daily actions with those values?"*

If you value kindness, for example, practicing small acts of kindness can infuse your life with a sense of purpose. If you value creativity, carving out time to paint, write, or perform music can reignite your inner flame.

Purpose anchors you, giving you the motivation to persevere when challenges arise.

Tactic #5: Reflective Practice

If resilience is a muscle, reflection is the workout routine. Set aside time—daily, weekly, or monthly—to check in with yourself. Ask questions like:

- **What challenges did I face recently, and how did I handle them?**
- **What worked well, and what could I do differently next time?**
- **Am I living in alignment with my values and goals?**
- **Where do I need extra support or self-care?**

Journaling can be particularly powerful here. By writing down your experiences, you create a record of your emotional journey, observe patterns in your reactions, and note improvements or recurring issues.

Over time, these reflections become a roadmap for your growth, helping you refine your resilience strategies.

Tactic #6: Seeking Connection and Support

Resilience doesn't mean going in alone. In fact, strong social ties are consistently linked to better mental health outcomes and improved stress management.

Whether confiding in a close friend, joining a support group, or consulting a therapist, reaching out can lighten the emotional load.

Sometimes, just having someone listen without judgment can be transformative, reminding you that you're not isolated in your struggles.

And remember, connection is a two-way street. Offering support to others—through volunteering, active listening, or small acts of kindness—can also bolster your own resilience.

There's something about lifting each other up that fortifies our emotional core.

Putting It All Together

Emotional resilience isn't a quick fix; it's a lifestyle.

It's about weaving together self-compassion, healthy habits, adaptability, a sense of purpose, reflective practice, and supportive relationships into a strong safety net for your emotional well-being.

When storms come—because they will—you have multiple layers of protection. Others can pick up the slack even if a few fail or feel insufficient.

Of course, building resilience is easier said than done.

There will be setbacks, days when you feel like you're right back where you started.

That's part of the process.

Each stumble provides a learning opportunity to recalibrate and grow stronger.

Over time, you'll look back and see how far you've come: waves that once knocked you off your feet now seem more manageable, and you'll realize that the ocean within you is broad, deep, and infinitely capable of renewal.

CONCLUSION TO CHAPTER 6

"Mastering Emotional Waves" is an ongoing practice—a blend of self-awareness, mindful choice, and strategic resilience-building.

In **Identifying Emotional Triggers**, we learned to spot the hidden switches that activate intense feelings, understanding that each trigger stems from past experiences or ingrained beliefs.

Recognizing these triggers gives you the power to anticipate emotional waves rather than be blindsided by them.

Then, in **Riding the Ups and Downs**, we discovered that emotions are natural and impermanent—like waves that rise and fall. Instead of denying or suppressing these feelings, you can surf them with greater skill, using mindfulness and healthy outlets to avoid being overwhelmed.

Whether it's anger, sadness, or anxiety, riding the wave means respecting the emotion's presence and allowing it to move through you until it dissipates.

Finally in **Emotional Resilience Tactics**, offered a toolkit for strengthening your overall capacity to weather life's storms.

Each tactic adds a layer of protection, from self-compassion to healthy routines, cognitive flexibility, and seeking meaningful connections.

The result isn't invincibility but a more profound confidence in your ability to navigate challenges and bounce back—like a sturdy ship that can sail even in rough waters.

As you integrate these insights into your life, remember that real change takes patience, practice, and self-compassion.

Nobody masters the art of emotional surfing overnight. You'll have good days when the waves feel small and manageable and more challenging days when it feels like you're being tossed around by a giant swell. Both experiences are valid and part of your growth.

From here, consider taking small, concrete steps—start that Trigger Tracking log, practice a brief "surfing" technique when you feel your next emotional rise, or explore one of the resilience tactics that resonates most with you.

The ocean of your emotions may never be completely calm (and wouldn't that be a bit boring if it were?), but with these tools, you'll be far less likely to drown in it.

Learning to master your emotional waves is one of the greatest gifts you can give yourself. It frees up mental energy, sharpens your focus, enriches your relationships, and helps you stress less—so you can truly, vibrantly **live more**.

And if you're ready to keep expanding your emotional toolkit, stay with us; there's much more to discover on this journey toward greater mindfulness, resilience, and joy.

You deserve every drop of it.

CHAPTER 7
HEALTHY BOUNDARIES, HAPPY LIFE

INTRODUCTION

Take a moment to imagine your life as a sprawling landscape—your personal kingdom—where you set the rules, define the borders and decide how visitors may or may not enter.

Now, picture what happens when no fences or gates are in sight: strangers might wander freely across your garden, trampling your flowers, uprooting your vegetable patch, and plucking your prized roses without a second thought.

That's precisely how life can feel when you lack clear, healthy boundaries. You're left vulnerable—exhausted from trying to guard your valuable inner world, but never quite sure where to draw the line.

Healthy boundaries act like a welcoming but well-defined fence. They don't necessarily shut everyone out or lock you in; instead, they create a safe perimeter that allows you to decide who and what is permitted into your mental and emotional space.

If you've ever felt unappreciated at work because you kept taking on extra tasks nobody else wanted or found yourself burned out by social events you never really wanted to attend, then you've experienced the consequences of flimsy or nonexistent boundaries. And if you're reading this chapter, chances are you're ready for a change.

Over the following few pages, we'll explore how establishing boundaries can profoundly impact your stress levels and overall quality of life.

We'll begin by looking at **Learning to Say "No"** (Subchapter 7.1)—that simple two-letter word that can feel as hard to pronounce as a tongue twister.

We'll delve into the fears and guilt that often keep us from declining demands and discover why saying "no" is crucial for preserving our time, energy, and mental health.

From there, we'll move on to **Respecting Your Own Limits** (Subchapter 7.2).

Even if you've mastered the art of telling others "no," it's another challenge to honor your boundaries.

We'll dive into the subtle ways we can self-sabotage by overextending ourselves, ignoring our needs, or downplaying our exhaustion.

You'll find tips to help you stay aligned with your personal values and cultivate a more nurturing relationship with yourself.

Finally, we'll explore **Social Interactions Without Burnout** (Subchapter 7.3), focusing on how to handle group settings, parties, friendships, and family gatherings in a way that leaves you feeling enriched rather than drained.

Many of us carry social obligations like we're weighed down by a fully loaded backpack: birthdays, weddings, networking events, family reunions—the list can feel endless.

But what if there's a way to participate in social life, enjoy genuine connections, and still guard your energy?

It turns out there is, and it starts with setting boundaries that protect both your sense of belonging and your need for rest.

If you're prone to people-pleasing or wish to magically add a few extra hours to your day, this chapter is for you.

Boundaries may sound like a harsh concept—especially if you fear disappointing others—but in truth, they can be liberating.

They allow you to show up more authentically, engage in meaningful activities, and ultimately stress less so you can *live more*. Ready to find out how?

Let's open the gate to a happier, healthier personal kingdom.

7.1 LEARNING TO SAY "NO"

Why "No" Can Feel So Impossible

You've probably heard it said that "No" is a complete sentence. Yet, for many of us, uttering that one little word can set off a storm of anxiety, guilt, or even a fear of rejection.

Maybe you worry about coming across as selfish. Maybe you dread confrontation.

Or perhaps you've been taught—directly or indirectly—that your worth depends on being agreeable, helpful, or easygoing.

Whatever the reason, you find yourself nodding "yes" when every fiber of your being wants to say "no."

Does any of this sound familiar? Picture a scenario: You're already juggling a hundred tasks, but your coworker says, "Hey, can you help me with this project?"

You sense your stress level rising to your eyeballs, yet somehow, the words "Sure, no problem!" slip out of your mouth.

Now, you're even more overwhelmed, resentful of the coworker, and frustrated with yourself.

But hey, at least you've avoided the awkwardness of turning them down, right?

The Hidden Costs of Saying "Yes" All the Time

Before we delve into strategies for comfortably saying "no," let's examine the cost of never doing so.

Consistently saying "yes" when you mean "no" can lead to:

- **Burnout**: Over-committing to tasks, events, and responsibilities leaves you chronically stressed and exhausted.

- **Resentment**: You might feel taken advantage of, even though you technically agreed to each request. This can result in simmering anger toward the person making the request and toward yourself for not speaking up.

- **Loss of Authenticity**: When you perpetually say "yes" out of fear or obligation, you deny your true feelings. Over time, you lose touch with your genuine desires and values, eroding your sense of self.

- **Diminished Quality of Work and Relationships**: With your energy spread thin, you can't give your best to the tasks or relationships that truly matter. You might become half-present everywhere rather than fully present somewhere.

The cumulative effect of these issues is an overarching feeling of depletion. You start to see life through a lens of obligation rather than passion, and that's not a recipe for joy or peace.

Redefining "No" as an Act of Respect—For Yourself and Others

Saying "no" isn't about being harsh or confrontational; it's about respecting the limits of your time, energy, and emotional bandwidth. It also respects the other person by offering clarity.

Think about it: if you grudgingly say "yes" and then do a rushed, resentful job, is that really the kind of help or presence that benefits anyone? Probably not.

When you honestly decline a request, you free that person to find a more willing and capable helper—or maybe discover they can handle the matter themselves.

Meanwhile, you uphold your own boundaries, preventing the buildup of resentment or burnout.

It's a win-win, even if it doesn't always feel that way at first.

Practical Strategies for Saying "No"

- **Start Small**: If you're chronically agreeable, practice "no" in low-stakes situations first. This might be declining an invitation to a minor social event you are not interested in. Once you see that the world doesn't end, you'll gain confidence for bigger "no's."
- **Be Brief and Honest**: When turning someone down, you don't owe them a 10-minute speech or a laundry list of excuses. A simple "I'm sorry, but I can't take this on

right now" often suffices. Over-explaining can invite negotiation.

- **Offer an Alternative (When Appropriate)**: If you genuinely want to help but can't do it as requested, you could say, "I can't attend the entire event, but I could contribute a dish," or "I can't tackle that full project, but I can review your final draft." This shows willingness without sacrificing your limits.

- **Practice "The Compassionate No"**: Sometimes it helps to express empathy: "I understand this is important to you, and I wish I could help, but I'm not able to commit right now." This acknowledges the other person's feelings while asserting your boundary.

- **Use Body Language**: Firm, calm body language (e.g., maintaining eye contact, speaking steadily) can make your "no" more believable and comfortable. If you look away or mumble, the other person might sense an opening to persuade you otherwise.

Dealing with the Aftermath

The first few times you say "no," you might feel guilty or worry you've disappointed someone. That's normal.

Overcoming this discomfort requires self-compassion.

Remember that it's okay to have personal boundaries, that you're not obligated to meet every demand, and that people will adapt. If the person reacts poorly—maybe they accuse you of being "selfish" or "inflexible"—try not to internalize their frustration.

Often, their anger stems from feeling inconvenienced, not from a genuine moral failing on their part.

A Quick Exercise: The "No" Journal

For a week, record each time you say "no" to a request or notice you *wanted* to say "no" but ended up saying "yes."

Write down how it felt in the moment and afterward. Note any patterns in your emotions or reactions from others.

Over time, you'll see that your "no" rarely causes the catastrophes you might have imagined, and your "yes" becomes more intentional, free of the old, anxious sense of obligation.

By learning to say "no," you reclaim a crucial piece of your mental and emotional real estate.

Sure, there may be bumps along the way—self-doubt, people's expectations, or the occasional guilt trip—but you'll also notice a liberating sense of having more room for what genuinely matters.

The next step? Ensuring you also uphold those boundaries for yourself is often a trickier endeavor.

Let's delve into that in the following subchapter.

7.2 RESPECTING YOUR OWN LIMITS

The Inner Critic vs. The Inner Caretaker

Saying "no" to external requests is one thing; respecting our own personal boundaries is another challenge entirely.

Think of it this way: Sometimes, the demands we struggle with don't come from friends, family, or coworkers but from internal pressure.

Perhaps you've told yourself, *"I must always be productive," "I should never skip a workout,"* or *"I can't take a day off if I'm not physically sick."*

While discipline can be healthy, endless self-imposed demands often lead to burnout.

It's like having a very stern boss who lives inside your head, pushing you to your limits without checking if you've had a break or a day off.

This is where the concept of the inner caretaker comes in. Your inner caretaker is the voice that gently reminds you it's okay to rest, to say "enough," to set realistic goals rather than chasing impossible perfection.

Unfortunately, for many of us, that caretaker's voice gets drowned out by the persistent inner critic, who loves to say things like, "You're just being lazy," or "Everyone else can handle more, so why can't you?"

The result is a cycle of over-commitment and self-flagellation.

Spotting Your Personal Overload Signals

To respect your own limits, you first have to recognize them.

Ever notice that you get a certain kind of headache when you're overworked or irritable when running on too little sleep?

These are your body's way of saying, *"Hey, something's not right here."* Other signals might include:

- **Chronic Fatigue**: Feeling worn down even after a whole night's sleep.
- **Loss of Enthusiasm**: Activities you typically enjoy start to feel like chores.
- **Heightened Anxiety**: Little problems trigger significant emotional reactions.
- **Physical Tension**: Tight shoulders, clenched jaw, or an upset stomach.
- **Trouble Focusing**: Difficulty maintaining concentration on tasks you usually breeze through.

Learning to tune into these signals is crucial. They're your internal "check engine" lights, advising you to slow down, refuel, or change course. Ignoring them can lead to bigger breakdowns—physical illness, severe burnout, or emotional crises.

Setting Micro-Boundaries with Yourself

Just as you set boundaries with others, you can also create micro-boundaries for your behaviors. Here are some examples:

- **Screen-Time Limits**: Decide that you'll stop checking work emails after 7 p.m. or won't scroll through social media past 10 p.m. This boundary protects your mental space and helps you wind down for better sleep.

- **Workday Breaks**: Schedule short breaks every couple of hours to stretch, grab a healthy snack, or simply breathe. Don't wait until you're utterly fried to step away.

- **Self-Care "Non-Negotiables"**: Identify a few daily practices—like a 10-minute walk, 15 minutes of reading for pleasure, or a quiet cup of tea—before bed that you commit to, no matter what.

- **Time Blocking**: Block off time in your calendar for tasks that matter to you personally—learning a new skill, exercising, or even daydreaming. This boundary ensures that your personal priorities get scheduled rather than forever postponed.

These micro-boundaries serve as small guardrails that prevent you from veering into the dangerous territory of overcommitment. They say, *"I value my well-being enough to carve out space and time for it."*

It might initially feel uncomfortable, especially if you're used to operating at full throttle.

But once you taste the benefits—better focus, improved mood, more creativity—you'll wonder why you ever lived without them.

Navigating Internal Resistance

You may still encounter internal resistance even when you know your limits intellectually.

You might think, *"But if I take a break, I'll fall behind,"* or, *"Everyone else seems to be able to handle this pace."* This is a classic case of comparing your backstage reality to someone else's highlight reel.

Remember, you don't see the private struggles, late-night stress, or hidden burnout others endure. Comparing your limits to theirs is neither fair nor realistic.

When resistance arises, try to engage with it compassionately.

Ask questions like: *"What am I afraid will happen if I respect my limits?"* or *"Is this fear based on reality or my own assumptions?"*

Often, you'll discover that your fears are manageable or even unfounded. Additionally, remind yourself that respecting your limits isn't a weakness; it's a sign of wisdom.

A well-rested, mentally stable version of you is far more effective and joyous than an overextended, perpetually frazzled version.

The Art of Downtime

In a culture that glorifies hustle, downtime can feel like a guilty pleasure or an act of defiance. But genuine downtime is essential for mental health, emotional resilience, and sustained creativity.

Whether curling up with a good book, hitting the gym for a leisurely workout, or daydreaming while sipping coffee, downtime refills your internal tank.

- **Plan It**: Schedule downtime in your calendar, just as you would a work meeting. This will make it a priority rather than an afterthought.
- **Unplug**: True downtime means stepping away from constant digital stimulation. Even a short break from screens can reset your mind.

- **Savor the Moment**: Instead of mentally running through your to-do list, focus on the enjoyment or relaxation you're experiencing. This mindfulness enhances the restorative power of your break.

A Quick Exercise: The "Personal Bill of Rights"

Sit down and write a "personal bill of rights" for yourself. Include statements like:
- "I have the right to take breaks when I'm tired."
- "I have the right to say 'no' to tasks that exceed my capacity."
- "I have the right to prioritize my mental health."
- "I have the right to change my mind if something no longer aligns with my well-being."

Keep this list visible on your desk, fridge, or phone. Whenever you're tempted to push yourself past your limits or deny your own needs, revisit these "rights" as a gentle reminder that you're allowed to take care of yourself.

Respecting your own limits is a cornerstone of healthy boundaries.

After all, how can we expect others to respect our boundaries if we keep ignoring them?

By doing this inner work—listening to your body, challenging your inner critic, and allowing yourself moments of rest—you ensure that your energy levels remain balanced and your zest for life stays intact.

That way, saying "yes" to something comes from genuine enthusiasm rather than frazzled obligation.

With these personal boundaries in place, let's move on to a context that often tests them to the max: social interactions.

In the following subchapter, we'll explore navigating gatherings, group outings, and even close relationships without sacrificing peace or health.

7.3 SOCIAL INTERACTIONS WITHOUT BURNOUT

The Paradox of Connection

Humans are social creatures. We crave companionship, laughter, and shared experiences.

Yet, ironically, socializing can become one of our most significant sources of stress—especially if we're dealing with crowded events, demanding social circles, or the pressure to always be "on."

Have you ever come home from a busy weekend feeling not rejuvenated but utterly spent, as if you need another weekend just to recuperate?

If so, you're not alone.

Balancing the desire for connection with the need for personal space can be tricky, but healthy boundaries make it possible.

Recognizing Social Overload

Social burnout can creep up on you. You may start noticing that you're dreading parties you used to enjoy or snapping at friends for minor annoyances.

Or perhaps you feel a sense of numbness in group settings—like you're physically present but emotionally checked out.

These symptoms suggest you might be hitting your social threshold.

Don't confuse social overload with disliking people or wanting to become a hermit.

Even extroverts can experience burnout when their calendar is too full of obligatory events and not enough meaningful connections.

The key is not about isolating yourself but curating your social life so it includes balanced, nourishing interactions.

The Power of Selective Socializing

One of the most effective ways to avoid social burnout is to be more intentional about your social choices.

This doesn't mean you must only ever spend time with your three best friends.

It just means deciding which events, relationships, and commitments enrich your life. Consider:

- **Quality over Quantity**: A deep, one-on-one coffee date with a close friend might be more fulfilling than attending a large gathering where you barely know anyone.

- **Different Circles, Different Energy**: Some social groups leave you uplifted and inspired; others might drain or trigger your insecurities. Recognizing this difference can guide you in deciding which invites to accept and which to decline.

- **Time Limits**: If you do decide to go to a big party or networking event, set a time boundary. For instance, plan to stay for two hours instead of all night. This approach helps you manage your energy and exit before running on empty.

Communicating Social Boundaries

It can feel awkward to tell someone, *"I'm going to leave early,"* or *"I need some alone time."* Still, the alternative—staying put until you're frazzled or resentful—tends to be far worse.

Most people will understand if you say, "I'd love to join for dinner, but I'll have to head out before the late-night festivities."

If they don't understand, that's often a reflection of their own issues, not a failing on your part.

Moreover, if you have friends or family who repeatedly pressure you to do more than you're comfortable with, remember that you have the right to stand firm.

Politely but firmly say, "I appreciate the invite, but I need to recharge tonight," or "I've got too much going on right now, so I have to pass."

You might be surprised at how often people respect a clear boundary—sometimes they're just used to you always saying "yes."

Navigating Family Gatherings

Family dynamics can be some of the trickiest waters to navigate. You might have relatives who expect you at every holiday event or guilt-trip you for leaving "too soon."

While it's wonderful to maintain strong family ties, that shouldn't come at the cost of your emotional well-being.

Here are a few tips:
- **Set Clear Expectations**: Let family members know how long you plan to stay or what role you can realistically play (e.g., you can bring a dessert but not host the entire meal).

- **Have an Exit Strategy**: If tensions run high (as they often do during big holidays), plan a polite way to leave before arguments start or exhaustion sets in.
- **Enlist Allies**: If you have supportive siblings or cousins, team up. Communicate your needs so they can help deflect any family pressure.

It's not about being rude but about recognizing that your emotional tank has limits.

A calm and collected you for a shorter duration is far better than a you who's around all day but stressed to the max.

Work and Networking Events

Another arena where boundaries can get murky is professional life.

The pressure to "show face" can be immense, from after-work happy hours to weekend conferences.

While networking has benefits, overdoing it can lead to the same kind of social fatigue you experience in personal settings. Consider:

- **Specific Goals**: Instead of milling around aimlessly at a networking event, identify one or two people or topics you genuinely want to explore. Make those connections, and then feel free to head out.
- **Rotate Downtime**: Schedule mini-breaks or alone time if the event spans multiple days. This is especially crucial for introverts, but even extroverts benefit from a mental reset.

- **Boundaries with Colleagues**: Be transparent if you need a mental health evening off. "I'm going to skip tonight's outing to recharge, but I'll be back in top form tomorrow" can go a long way in maintaining professional relationships without sacrificing yourself.

Social Media Boundaries

Social interaction isn't limited to face-to-face encounters in today's connected world. Social media can become a 24/7 gathering that can deplete your mental energy if you're constantly plugged in.

Establishing boundaries around your online presence—limiting how often you check notifications or turn off your phone during certain hours—can prevent digital burnout. Remember, it's okay not to respond immediately to every message or occasionally skip browsing your feed if it's causing stress.

A Quick Exercise: The Social Recharge Scale

Rate how each social interaction (or event) makes you feel on a scale from -5 (draining) to +5 (energizing).

Then:

1. **Notice Patterns**: Are there types of events consistently in the negative zone? Could you reduce them or make them more manageable?
2. **Schedule Based on Energy**: If an event is likely a -4, plan a rest day or a self-care evening afterward. If something is a +4, you might seek more of that interaction.

3. **Adjust Over Time**: Your preferences might shift as you grow or your circumstances change. Periodically reassess to ensure your social calendar aligns with your current reality.

By taking a more mindful, selective approach to socializing, you can maintain fulfilling connections without succumbing to burnout.

You'll also learn that true friends understand and respect your boundaries—they want you at your best, not depleted and resentful.

And those who don't respect your limits? That's a sign you might need to reassess their role in your life.

CONCLUSION TO CHAPTER 7

Healthy Boundaries, Happy Life might sound like a catchy slogan, but it captures an essential truth: boundaries—both external and internal—create the conditions in which you can thrive.

In **Learning to Say "No"**, we discovered how a two-letter word can be the gateway to reclaiming your time, reducing overwhelm, and preventing resentment.

Yes, it can feel awkward or guilt-inducing initially, but each time you choose "no" over a forced "yes," you're practicing self-respect.

We then moved to **Respecting Your Own Limits**, exploring how we can overextend ourselves without external pressure.

Our inner critic can be as demanding as any boss or friend, pushing us to achieve more, do more, and be more—often at the expense of our health.

By learning to recognize your personal overload signals, setting micro-boundaries, and carving out restorative downtime, you honor your most important relationship with yourself.

Finally, in **Social Interactions Without Burnout**, we tackled the delicate dance of managing social obligations.

Whether it's a family gathering, networking event, or impromptu hangout, mindful boundary-setting can help you balance your craving for connection with your need for rest.

The result? More authentic interactions, less obligatory mingling, and a calendar that reflects your true priorities.

Throughout this chapter, we've returned to one core idea: boundaries are not walls that shut people out; they're fences with gates, allowing you to welcome the right energies into your world while keeping chaos at bay.

By selectively choosing where to invest your time and energy, you free yourself from endless obligations and start to live in alignment with your deepest values.

That alignment, in turn, reduces stress and heightens your sense of fulfillment.

Are there times you'll slip up? Of course. You might say "yes" again when you want to say "no," or you might ignore your signals and push too far.

That's where self-compassion swoops in. Each misstep is an opportunity to learn, refine, and grow. Over time, your boundaries become second nature.

This invisible support system helps you stand tall and remain clear-headed in a world filled with requests, invitations, and expectations.

So, here's your gentle challenge: over the next week, pick one boundary to solidify—maybe it's declining a small favor you truly can't handle, leaving a party earlier to catch a quiet evening at home, or pledging to turn off work emails by a particular hour.

Notice how it feels, and pay attention to any emotional ripple effects.

My guess? You'll find that most people adapt just fine, and the sky doesn't fall.

In fact, you may experience a bit of joy, relief, or pride at realizing you're more in control of your life than you thought.

And that's what **stress less, live more** is all about: freeing your time, energy, and emotional bandwidth for the pursuits and people that truly matter to you.

After all, life is far too precious to juggle obligations that drain rather than sustain us.

With healthy boundaries, you position yourself to fully embrace the experiences that light you up—and isn't that what living is really about?

CHAPTER 8
NOURISH YOUR BODY, NOURISH YOUR SOUL

INTRODUCTION

Picture this: You wake up feeling groggy, hit the snooze button three times, and then stumble through your morning routine in a blur.

By midday, you're running on caffeine and sheer willpower, nibbling on whatever snack bar you found at the bottom of your bag, only to realize at 3 p.m. that you're too jittery to focus and hungry to function. Sound familiar?

For many of us, taking care of our physical selves often falls to the bottom of the priority list—especially when we're stressed or overloaded.

Yet, paradoxically, when we neglect our bodies, our stress levels skyrocket, our emotional resilience wanes, and our overall sense of well-being takes a nosedive.

It's like driving without putting gas in the tank or checking the oil.

You can only run on fumes for so long before something breaks down.

In this chapter, we'll delve into the idea that nourishing your body isn't just about fueling a machine.

It's also about nourishing your soul—tending to the parts of you that crave vitality, joy, and rest.

We'll start by examining **Stress-Less Eating Habits** (Subchapter 8.1), exploring how mindful and balanced approaches to food can profoundly impact your emotional state.

Next, we'll shift gears to **The Power of Movement** (Subchapter 8.2), looking at how exercise and physical activity can be your secret weapons in the fight against stress.

Finally, we'll end with **Restful Sleep Essentials** (Subchapter 8.3) because let's face it. Even the best diet and exercise regimen will get you so far without proper rest.

Consider this chapter your guide to building a healthy foundation supporting **less stress** and **more life**.

These aren't rigid rules or crash-course commands. They're invitations.

Invitations to listen to your body, to cultivate a kinder relationship with it, and, in the process, to give your soul the nourishment it's been quietly asking for.

After all, you deserve more than just "getting by." You deserve to thrive.

8.1 STRESS-LESS EATING HABITS

The Emotional Side of Eating

Raise your hand if you've ever turned to a pint of ice cream after a bad day or mindlessly munched on potato chips while binge-watching your favorite show. (My hand is up, too!)

Food isn't just about nutrition—it carries a hefty emotional load. We celebrate with it, we grieve with it, and sometimes, we rely on it as our go-to stress reliever. No wonder our relationship with food can get tangled in guilt, anxiety, or even shame.

But here's a comforting thought: you're not weak or "bad" for having emotional ties to food.

Thanks to survival mechanisms passed down from our hunter-gatherer days, our brains are wired to find comfort in eating, especially sweet or fatty foods.

However, in our modern world—where snacks are abundant, and stress is high—this biological tendency can backfire, leaving us with health issues or increased stress levels due to poor dietary choices.

The Mindful Eating Approach

Mindful eating offers a refreshing alternative to mindless munching. Instead of scarfing down your lunch while scrolling through emails, you pause and genuinely taste each bite.

You notice the flavors, textures, and aromas of your meal. It sounds too simple, but solid research is behind this approach.

Eating more slowly and intentionally gives your brain and gut time to register satisfaction, which can prevent overeating and reduce post-meal energy crashes.

1. **Pause Before You Dig In**: Take a breath, look at your plate, and appreciate the food in front of you. Where did it come from? How was it prepared? This small moment of gratitude can shift your mindset from frantic to thankful.
2. **Chew Thoroughly**: Your grandmother's advice still holds. Chewing more thoroughly breaks down food for better digestion and slows your overall pace, making each meal feel more fulfilling.
3. **Check-In Mid-Meal**: Halfway through your meal, put your fork down and ask yourself, "Am I still hungry? How does my body feel?" If you're satisfied, you can decide whether to continue eating or save the rest for later. Yes, leftovers are a thing—and they're glorious.
4. **Savor the Experience**: Focus on the flavors, aromas, and textures. When your mind drifts off to worry about tomorrow's deadlines, gently bring it back to your plate. This mini mindfulness exercise helps you stay grounded in the present.

Balancing Nutrients Without the Drama

The word "diet" often comes with a slew of negative connotations—restriction, deprivation, maybe even failure if you've tried and abandoned multiple fad diets in the past.

Stressless eating is less about "dieting" and more about **balance** and **nourishment**.

While each person's nutritional needs vary, some general guidelines can help keep stress in check:
- **Complex Carbs**: Whole grains, fruits, and vegetables give you steady energy and support mood-regulating neurotransmitters like serotonin.
- **Protein**: Lean meats, beans, lentils, and nuts provide essential amino acids and stabilize blood sugar.
- **Healthy Fats**: Avocados, olive oil, and fatty fish like salmon are great for brain function and can help reduce stress-related inflammation.
- **Hydration**: Water is often overlooked but crucial for clear thinking and overall bodily function.

The point isn't to become a nutrition purist who never touches dessert.

It's about nurturing a general framework that lets you enjoy indulgences without guilt, knowing you're fueling your body—and, by extension, your mind—for the long haul.

Emotional Eating vs. Self-Care Eating

When stress hits, emotional eating can appear like the quickest fix for comfort—think salty fries after a tough day. But the relief is often short-lived, followed by regret or a stomachache.

Contrast this with self-care eating, where you might still choose a comforting meal—but from a place of kindness, not desperation. For example, a hearty bowl of homemade soup filled with veggies and a sprinkle of cheese.

One trick is to **pause** when a craving hits. Ask yourself: "Am I hungry, or am I anxious, lonely, or bored?"

If you're genuinely hungry, eat a balanced snack or meal. If it's an emotional craving, consider an alternate form of self-care—like a warm bath, a brisk walk, or calling a friend.

If you still want that scoop of ice cream afterward, you'll likely savor it more without the added baggage of guilt.

A Quick Exercise: The "Three-Breath Check-In"

Before any meal or snack, try this:

1. Take a **deep breath** in and out, noticing any tension in your body.
2. Take a **second breath**, focusing on the sense of hunger or fullness in your stomach.
3. Take a **third breath**, asking yourself what your body needs—nourishment, comfort, or perhaps simply hydration.

It might feel silly initially, but this tiny ritual can realign you with your body's signals, helping you avoid unconscious, stress-induced feeding frenzies.

By cultivating stress-less eating habits, you're doing more than just "watching what you eat."

You're fostering a kinder, more intuitive relationship with food that supports your energy levels, helps regulate mood, and frees you from the diet-guilt-stress cycle.

Once you've got this aspect humming, it's time to think about how physical movement can elevate your mental state.

8.2 THE POWER OF MOVEMENT

Why Exercise Beats Couch Lock (Even When You're Tired)

Close your eyes and picture how you feel after a good workout. You may be sweaty, and your muscles might be sore.

Still, there's also that undeniable sense of accomplishment and an energized buzz coursing through you. It's like your body's version of a "high five."

Now compare that to how you feel after a marathon session of binge-watching TV on the couch—sluggish, maybe a bit antsy, and possibly more stressed if you've spent the entire time ruminating on your to-do list. We've all been there, thinking, *"I should exercise... but... Netflix."*

Here's a little secret: **movement** might be our most underused yet effective stress reliever. When you get your heart rate up, you release endorphins—those feel-good chemicals that help combat stress hormones like cortisol.

Plus, physical activity triggers the production of neurotransmitters like serotonin and dopamine, which can help stabilize mood and foster resilience.

Ditching the "All or Nothing" Mentality

One of the biggest obstacles to getting more active is the belief that exercise has to be hardcore or time-consuming—endless hours at the gym, intense HIIT routines, or half-marathons every weekend.

If you love that, great! But if you don't, it can be a massive barrier. The truth is, **any** movement is better than no movement.

A 20-minute walk around the neighborhood or a short YouTube yoga session can do wonders for clearing your mind and loosening stiff muscles.

- **Micro-Workouts**: Try taking the stairs instead of the elevator, or do a quick set of squats while waiting for your coffee to brew. These tiny bursts of activity add up over time.
- **Movement Snacks**: Just as you might have a healthy snack when you're peckish, think of taking a "movement snack" every couple of hours—like walking around the block or doing a few stretches in your living room.
- **Active Hobbies**: Dancing, gardening, hiking, playing a sport—whatever floats your boat and gets your body moving. The key is finding something you genuinely enjoy so it feels fun rather than a chore.

Mind-Body Exercises: A Two-for-One Deal

Yoga, Pilates, and tai chi aren't just exercise routines; they're mindfulness practices in motion. They connect breath to movement, teaching you to pay attention to how your body feels and how your mind responds.

If you're new to mind-body exercises, consider starting with beginner-friendly yoga flows on YouTube or a local studio's intro class. You might be surprised how effectively these practices can calm your muscles and racing thoughts.

- **Yoga**: Beyond flexibility, yoga can help regulate stress responses, improve sleep quality, and strengthen core muscles. Bonus points if you can handle a few face plants while learning crow pose—humor is excellent stress relief.

- **Pilates**: Think of it like a core-centric, controlled approach to movement. Great for improving posture and balance, which can boost confidence and reduce body aches that contribute to stress.
- **Tai Chi or Qigong**: These slow, flowing practices emphasize balance and intentional breathing. They are perfect for unwinding in a meditative way while gently moving your body.

The Joy Factor

Ever notice how kids run around the playground, giggling and shrieking with delight as they chase each other?

For them, movement is inherently fun.

Yet, as adults, we often lose that sense of playfulness, labeling exercise "work" or "punishment."

Reclaiming the joy factor can significantly reduce stress around working out.

Whether blasting your favorite dance tunes in your living room, joining a recreational sports league, or even hula hooping in your backyard, infusing fun into movement keeps you motivated and relaxed.

Listening to Your Body

While movement is essential, it's equally important not to push yourself to exhaustion or injury.

There's a sweet spot between challenging yourself and respecting your limits.

Suppose you're dealing with chronic stress or mental health struggles. In that case, intense workouts might sometimes exacerbate anxiety or burnout if you're not mindful.

Pay attention to how you feel during and after your chosen activity. If you notice you're more anxious or physically drained, dial down the intensity or try a gentler exercise until you find the right balance.

A Quick Exercise: "Movement Mood Map"

1. **List Your Top 3 Favorite Activities**: Anything from jogging with your dog to dancing around your kitchen.
2. **Next to Each Activity, Write How It Makes You Feel**: Energized, calm, playful, empowered—whatever emotional responses come up.
3. **Match Activity to Mood**: Which activities would best help you decompress when anxious? When you're feeling sluggish, which might pump you up?
4. **Plan Weekly**: Based on your schedule and typical mood dips (like that Wednesday slump), plan at least one or two sessions of your chosen activity.

Making movement a regular part of your routine—without the all-or-nothing mindset—gives you a powerful stress relief strategy and emotional resilience. You also set the stage for a healthier, happier you.

So, you're eating more mindfully and moving your body in good ways.

Restful sleep is another cornerstone to address for a well-rounded, stress-less lifestyle.

8.3 RESTFUL SLEEP ESSENTIALS

When Counting Sheep Doesn't Cut It

We've all been there—lying in bed, staring at the ceiling, counting sheep (or the ticking seconds on the clock), desperately hoping for sleep to come.

Meanwhile, tomorrow's anxieties swirl through your mind like a never-ending carousel.

If you've ever felt the frustration of tossing and turning until the wee hours, you know how sleep deprivation amplifies stress.

Suddenly, minor obstacles morph into towering challenges, and your emotional resilience plummets.

Quality sleep is like hitting the "reset" button on your brain.

During deep stages of sleep, your body repairs tissues consolidates memories and regulates hormones crucial for stress management.

You rob yourself of this nightly recharge when you skimp on sleep—whether by choice or circumstance.

Over time, chronic sleep deprivation can lead to increased cortisol levels, impaired concentration, mood swings, and even a weakened immune system.

Setting the Stage for Better Sleep

We often treat sleep like an afterthought that should happen naturally after a long day. But if stress or insomnia have entered the picture, you may need to make sleep more of a priority and ritual. Consider these foundational steps:

- **Consistent Bedtime & Wake-Up**: Your body loves routines. Going to bed and waking up roughly the same time each day helps stabilize your internal clock, making it easier to fall asleep and wake up feeling rested.

- **Dim the Lights and Power Down Screens**: Blue light from phones, tablets, and computers can disrupt melatonin production (the hormone that signals your body it's time to sleep). Avoid bright screens an hour before bed, or use a blue-light filter if you must use your devices.

- **Cool, Dark, and Quiet**: Your bedroom should be a sleep sanctuary. If noise is an issue, consider earplugs or a white noise machine. Blackout curtains or a sleep mask can help if streetlights or early sunrise floods your room.

- **Be Mindful of Caffeine and Alcohol**: Caffeine can linger in your system for several hours, potentially keeping you awake. While alcohol might help you doze off initially, it can disrupt later stages of sleep, leading to poor quality rest.

The Wind-Down Routine

Ever notice how children often have a bedtime routine—bath, storytime, lullaby—yet adults typically crash whenever they can? It's no wonder kids often sleep more soundly.

A pre-sleep ritual cues your brain that it's time to shift into rest mode. Your wind-down routine might include:

- **Light Reading**: Choose something relaxing or entertaining, not a suspenseful page-turner that keeps you anxious or alert.

- **Gentle Stretching or Yoga**: Simple poses like a child's pose or legs up the wall can calm your nervous system.
- **Journaling**: Offload worries, capture gratitudes, or write about the day's triumphs and challenges. This mental "download" can prevent your brain from ruminating once the lights go out.
- **Soothing Music or Guided Meditation**: Low-volume, calming tunes or a short guided relaxation track can help ease tense muscles and anxious thoughts.

Taming the Midnight Mind Race

Even with a stellar bedtime routine, you might still face nights when your brain won't shut up.

You may be replaying a stressful conversation or worrying about tomorrow's tasks.

A few strategies can help:
- **Keep a Notepad Handy**: Jot down whatever's circling your mind—appointments, random ideas, concerns. This symbolic "offloading" can reassure your brain that you won't forget anything important.
- **Try 4-7-8 Breathing**: Inhale for a count of four, hold for seven and exhale for eight. This technique can slow your heart rate and shift your focus from anxious thoughts to the soothing rhythm of your breath.
- **Body Scan Meditation**: Start at your toes and work up, mentally relaxing each body part. This fosters a more profound sense of relaxation and distracts you from racing thoughts.

- **Get Out of Bed if Needed**: If you've been awake for 20 minutes, get up, do something calm (like reading or light stretching), and only return to bed when you feel genuinely drowsy. This trains your brain to associate your bed with sleep, not restless tossing.

The Nap Debate

Naps can be a double-edged sword. A short "power nap" (20–30 minutes) can refresh you, boost your mood, and reduce stress.

But longer naps, especially later in the day, might interfere with nighttime sleep.

If napping regularly disrupts your sleep schedule, experiment with a shorter nap or skip it altogether.

A Quick Exercise: The "Goodnight Gratitude" Practice

Before you drift off, list three things you're grateful for that day. They don't have to be monumental—a kind text from a friend, a pleasant walk, or a delicious snack.

By focusing on the positive, you shift your mental state from worry or frustration to a calmer sense of appreciation.

This gentle rewiring can make it easier to drift into restorative sleep.

CONCLUSION TO CHAPTER 8

"Nourish Your Body, Nourish Your Soul" might sound like a catchy phrase you'd see on a wellness blog, but it's truly the cornerstone of a life with less stress and more joy.

We started by exploring **Stress-Less Eating Habits**, recognizing that food is more than mere calories.

It's emotional, cultural, and deeply personal.

By approaching eating with mindfulness—replacing guilt with gratitude and deprivation with balance—you foster a kinder relationship with your plate (and yourself).

Then, in **The Power of Movement**, we saw how integral physical activity is for physical health and emotional well-being.

Whether it's a leisurely stroll around the block, a spirited dance session in your living room, or a structured workout routine at the gym, movement can zap stress hormones and flood your brain with endorphins.

And it doesn't need to be intense or time-consuming; even micro-workouts and playful activities can do the trick.

Finally, we explored the realm of **Restful Sleep Essentials**. Sleep is where your body rebuilds and your mind re-centers.

It's the nightly therapy session your brain needs to process the day's events and prepare for tomorrow.

You safeguard this precious resource by honoring a consistent bedtime, crafting a wind-down routine, and using techniques to calm the midnight mind race.

All these facets—eating, moving, and sleeping—work together like a symphony.

When one is out of tune, the entire composition can suffer, leading to heightened stress and diminished resilience.

But when you nourish yourself on all three levels, you create a harmony that resonates throughout your days, brightening your mood, sharpening your focus, and giving you the emotional fortitude to face life's ups and downs.

Of course, no one's perfect at this 24/7. There will be days you stress about a bag of cookies, skip your workout, and stay up too late worrying.

That's life.

The goal is not perfection but awareness and self-compassion. You can gently guide yourself using this chapter's tools and insights whenever you notice you're veering off track.

Over time, these healthy habits become second nature, forming a sturdy base to build a life of greater ease, confidence, and fulfillment.

So here's your invitation: pick one small change from each subchapter—maybe a mindful breathing moment before meals, a 10-minute daily walk, and a screen-free wind-down for sleep.

Try them out for a week.

Notice how your body and mind respond.

You might be pleasantly surprised to find how these simple shifts can ease the weight of daily stress and open up more space for living—genuinely **living**—each day.

CHAPTER 9
PRODUCTIVE WITHOUT THE PRESSURE

INTRODUCTION

Has your mind ever felt like a traffic jam at rush hour—horns blaring, cars honking, everybody rushing to get somewhere but nobody really moving forward?

Maybe you're juggling deadlines, personal errands, and your dog's vet appointment (which you keep forgetting to schedule) while telling yourself, *"I really need to be more productive."*

If you've ever felt the weight of that pressure, this chapter is for you.

We live in a world that idolizes productivity. "Hustle culture" shouts at us to do more, earn more, and achieve more—often with a complete disregard for our mental and emotional well-being.

Ironically, the more we stress about productivity, the less capable we become of getting things done.

Anxiety turns into procrastination or frantic busyness, which is neither efficient nor satisfying.

So, how do we find a gentler path to productivity that doesn't involve late-night panic attacks or guilt-ridden weekends spent glued to our screens?

We'll start by exploring **Time Management Basics** (Subchapter 9.1) because, let's face it: if our days have no structure, they can easily unravel into a swirl of unfinished tasks and mental chaos. We'll look at defining our priorities without living by a dictatorial schedule.

From there, we'll dive into **Focus and Flow** (Subchapter 9.2), uncovering the secrets behind tapping into that almost magical mental state where work feels rewarding and pleasurable.

Finally, we'll explore **Gentle Accountability** (Subchapter 9.3), where you'll discover ways to stay on track without shaming or punishing yourself when life doesn't go according to plan.

The big takeaway? Productivity does *not* have to be synonymous with stress.

In fact, the best kind of productivity emerges when we're calm, centered, and mindful—when we're truly present with whatever task or project is in front of us. That's where we feel engaged, alive, and surprisingly efficient.

So, let's pour a soothing cup of tea or coffee and settle in to explore how to be productive without drowning in pressure.

9.1 TIME MANAGEMENT BASICS

More Than Just a To-Do List

Time management might sound as exciting as reorganizing your sock drawer, but it's the linchpin of a balanced life.

It's not just about scribbling tasks on a sticky note; it's about designing your day to make room for your obligations and joys.

Think about it: How often do you rush through your morning routine, promising yourself you'll exercise *tomorrow*?

Or how many times do you agree to back-to-back commitments, only to end up resentful and exhausted?

We all have 24 hours each day, which is 1,440 minutes.

Ironically, those minutes can feel unbelievably sparse if we don't use them wisely—or they can expand like the endless horizon, granting us space to breathe, think, and create.

Good time management is less about rigidity and more about clarity.

What truly matters? What can wait? And how can you protect your energy so you're not pouring from an empty cup?

Prioritization: The Secret Sauce

Ever find yourself staring at a to-do list the length of a novel, feeling so overwhelmed that you decide to scroll through social media instead?

In those moments, the problem isn't laziness—it's indecision.

You might not start at all if you don't know *where* to start.

That's where prioritization swoops in like a superhero. It's the process of ranking tasks by their importance and urgency.

A classic method is the "Eisenhower Matrix," which categorizes tasks into four quadrants:

- **Urgent and Important**: Requires immediate attention (e.g., a work deadline today, a sick pet needing a vet appointment).

- **Important but Not Urgent**: Vital tasks that help you achieve long-term goals but aren't on fire right now (e.g., learning a new skill, working on a side passion).

- **Urgent but Not Important**: Tasks that clamor for attention but may not contribute much to your personal or professional growth (e.g., some emails, small requests from others).

- **Not Urgent and Not Important**: Time-fillers or distractions (like random social media browsing or re-checking Netflix recommendations for the millionth time).

The goal? Spend as much time as possible on important things—both urgent and non-urgent—and minimize the rest.

By identifying which tasks truly matter to you and which are just "busy work," you can channel your energy more effectively.

Suddenly, your day feels more manageable. You realize that you don't have to do *everything* at once; you just have to do the *right things* at the right time.

Time Blocking for Sanity

Some folks thrive with a loose schedule, while others prefer more structure. Time **blocking** might become your new best friend if you lean toward the latter. With time blocking, you divide your day into specific chunks, each dedicated to a particular type of task. For example:

- **8:00–9:00 a.m.**: Morning routine (breakfast, light reading, journaling).
- **9:00–11:00 a.m.**: Deep work (focus on your most important project).
- **11:00–12:00 p.m.**: Emails and administrative tasks.
- **12:00–1:00 p.m.**: Lunch and a short walk.
- **1:00–3:00 p.m.**: Meetings or collaborative work.
- **3:00–4:00 p.m.**: Catch up on smaller tasks or wrap up any pending items.
- **4:00–5:00 p.m.**: Buffer time or personal errands.

Of course, your schedule will vary based on your job or lifestyle, but the concept remains. The advantage of time blocking is that you don't have to constantly decide what to do next—each block is pre-assigned.

This structure can reduce decision fatigue and help you stay grounded. Remember, it's not about perfect adherence; it's about guiding your day so you're less likely to feel adrift.

The Pomodoro Technique: Focus on Short Spurts

If you struggle with staying on task for long periods, the **Pomodoro Technique** might be your saving grace.

Named after the tomato-shaped kitchen timer, it's a simple process:
1. Choose a task.
2. Set a timer for 25 minutes (one "Pomodoro").
3. Work on the task with complete focus until the timer rings.
4. Take a short 5-minute break.
5. After four Pomodoros, take a more extended break of 15–30 minutes.

This approach does wonders for people prone to distractions or mental fatigue. Breaking tasks into small, concentrated chunks makes it easier to start—and continue—working.

You also get regular breaks to stand up, stretch, or glance at your phone guilt-free, knowing your next work sprint is just around the corner.

Flexibility Matters

While these techniques can be life-changing, beware of turning them into a new source of pressure. You can adapt or skip them on days that don't cooperate with your plans.

Feeling under the weather? You may need a slower pace. Suddenly, got an unexpected task from your boss? Adjust your blocks accordingly.

Time management is like dancing with the flow of daily life, not marching in a strict parade.

Moreover, the emotional aspect of time management should be considered. How do you handle the guilt when you fail to cross everything off your list?

Do you berate yourself or practice self-compassion, acknowledging that some days are more challenging than others?

This is the invisible layer of time management—learning to be kind to yourself so you don't spiral into a stress frenzy whenever your schedule doesn't go perfectly.

A Quick Exercise: The Nightly Review

Before bed, take five minutes to reflect on your day. Ask yourself:

- What went well today? (I think you handled a tricky email conversation with grace.)
- What could be improved tomorrow? (Perhaps you spent too much time on social media between tasks.)
- What are the top three things I want to accomplish tomorrow?

Jot your answers down in a journal or digital note. This brief reflection helps you see your progress and prepares your mind to tackle the next day's goals with clarity.

Over time, this habit can drastically reduce the morning scramble of *"Where do I even begin?"*

With time management basics under your belt, you'll find it easier to create pockets of focus and relaxation—setting the stage for that magical state we call "flow."

Let's explore that in the following subchapter.

9.2 FOCUS AND FLOW

The Elusive State of Flow

Have you ever been so absorbed in a task that time seemed to evaporate? When you finally looked up, two hours had flown by, and you were surprised by how much you'd accomplished without feeling mentally drained?

That, my friend, is **flow**—a term coined by psychologist Mihaly Csikszentmihalyi.

Flow is that sweet spot where your skills match the challenge, you're neither bored nor overwhelmed, and your concentration is so deep you forget about the clock (and maybe even your phone).

Flow can make work feel like play. It can transform mundane tasks into engaging puzzles, turning creative projects into joyful adventures.

Yet, in a world of endless notifications and distractions, finding flow can feel like chasing a unicorn. Here's how to make it more attainable:

Taming Distractions

We live in an attention economy. Countless apps, ads, and social feeds want your eyeballs, and your smartphone's constant pings can feel like a toddler tugging at your pant leg—relentless. If you're going to cultivate flow, you have to set boundaries around distractions.

- **Digital Decluttering**: Turn off non-essential notifications. Consider placing your phone in "Do Not Disturb" mode during focused work sessions. Create separate browser profiles—one for productive tasks and another for recreational browsing—so you're not tempted by your email inbox every time you open a new tab.

- **Physical Environment**: If your workspace is littered with half-empty coffee cups, random notes, and expired coupons from three months ago, your mind might subconsciously feel as cluttered as your desk. Tidy up. A clear space can encourage a clear mind.

Finding the Right Challenge Level

Flow is most likely to occur when a task is challenging enough to hold your interest but not so hard that it freaks you out. If your work is too easy, you'll get bored; if it's too tough, you'll get anxious. The key is to adjust the difficulty as you go:

- **Too Easy?** Introduce a small constraint or a personal deadline. For instance, if writing a report is a breeze, challenge yourself to finish a section by a certain time or try a new writing style to spark interest.
- **Too Hard?** Break the task into smaller steps, or seek help. Reducing the skill-challenge gap can help you reach that sweet zone of total absorption.

Rituals for Entering Flow

Sometimes, you need a ceremonial gateway to slip into flow. Athletes have pre-game routines. Musicians tune their instruments. Writers might light a candle or brew a cup of tea before typing the first sentence. These rituals signal your brain that it's "go time." They might be tiny—like doing a brief stretch or playing a specific instrumental track every time you start coding. But over time, these triggers can condition you to slide more effortlessly into deep focus.

Embracing Single-Tasking

In a society that worships multitasking, embracing single-tasking can feel almost rebellious.

However, research shows that true multitasking (trying to do two complex tasks simultaneously) is largely a myth.

We're really doing "task-switching," and our brains pay a heavy toll each time we shift focus.

Single-tasking—fully immersing yourself in one task at a time—makes it far easier to find flow.

You'll likely do better work, and you'll do it faster because your cognitive energy isn't splintered across multiple fronts.

Handling Interruptions with Grace

Even the best-laid plans can be thwarted by an unexpected phone call, a knock on the door, or your own racing thoughts.

When an interruption comes, respond calmly instead of snapping into frustration.

If someone needs your immediate attention, address it if it's urgent. If it's not urgent, ask if they can connect later or politely schedule a quick meeting at a designated time slot.

Afterward, don't beat yourself up if it takes a few minutes to recenter.

Gently guide yourself back into the task, maybe with a mini ritual—a deep breath, a quick stretch, or re-reading the last thing you wrote to regain context.

The Afterglow of Flow

Flow isn't just about productivity; it's about well-being.

You often feel a pleasant buzz of satisfaction when you finish a flow session.

You may notice that your stress levels have dropped, replaced by a sense of accomplishment and creative fulfillment.

Over time, chasing healthy doses of flow can turn work (or personal projects) into meaningful experiences rather than necessary chores.

Flow isn't always guaranteed, even when you set the perfect conditions. Some days, your mind will be too frazzled or your environment too chaotic. That's okay.

Striving for flow is about increasing the odds, not demanding perfection.

The magic happens when you treat focus like a skill to be honed rather than a fleeting gift from the muse of productivity.

A Quick Exercise: Micro-Flow Moments

Not every task warrants a multi-hour deep dive. Sometimes, you just want a snippet of flow.

Pick a small activity—maybe washing dishes, tidying a corner of your desk, or organizing a digital folder.

Challenge yourself to focus solely on that task for five minutes.

Turn off distractions, notice details (the smell of soap, the texture of objects), and allow yourself to be fully present.

Even a short burst of micro-flow can leave you feeling calmer and more centered, a perfect antidote to the modern epidemic of scatterbrain.

Once you've gained insight into time management and flow, there's just one more ingredient to ensure you stay consistent and accountable—minus the self-judgment or impossible demands we often place on ourselves.

That's where **Gentle Accountability** enters the picture.

9.3 GENTLE ACCOUNTABILITY

The Problem with Extreme Self-Criticism

Does this scenario ring a bell? You set an ambitious goal—to complete a creative project or finally clear out that closet—only to fall behind schedule.

Suddenly, your inner critic storms in, calling you lazy, unmotivated, or hopeless. You feel so demoralized that you avoid the task altogether, sinking into guilt or procrastination.

In a culture that prizes achievement, self-criticism often masquerades as "motivation." But in reality, it can strip away your enthusiasm, leaving a trail of shame and inaction.

We need accountability to move forward—that gentle nudge that says, *"Hey, you committed to this. Let's see it through."*

But accountability doesn't have to be harsh or punishing. It can be supportive, loving, and, yes, even fun.

The Buddy System

One effective way to stay accountable is to **team up with someone you trust**—a friend, colleague, or relative with goals they want to accomplish.

Arrange weekly check-ins over coffee or via text, updating each other on progress. These aren't guilt sessions; they're supportive chats designed to help you notice what's working, what's not, and how to adjust.

The mere fact that someone else knows your plans can be a powerful motivator to follow through—even if you're only trying to do something as simple as drinking more water or reading a chapter of a book daily.

Setting S.M.A.R.T. Goals

You've probably heard of **S.M.A.R.T. goals**: Specific, Measurable, Achievable, Relevant, and Time-bound.

They exist for a reason. Vague aspirations like "I want to be more organized" can flounder, as you have no concrete way to measure success.

In contrast, "I will organize my workspace by decluttering my desk drawers for 20 minutes every weekday for two weeks" is far more tangible. When your goals are this clear, tracking progress and staying focused is easier.

But remember, "Achievable" is part of the acronym for a good reason. Overly ambitious goals are like a guaranteed recipe for self-criticism when reality hits.

Choose something that challenges you without overwhelming you. And give yourself permission to revise your goals if life throws you a curveball.

Flexibility is a hallmark of gentle accountability.

Celebrating Small Wins

Modern life often feels like a never-ending race, with the finish line perpetually moving.

That's why celebrating **small wins** is crucial. Did you complete a challenging report? Did you manage to meditate three days in a row? Did you resist checking your phone during a focused work session? Applaud yourself!

These victories, however minor they might seem, fuel positive momentum. They reinforce the belief that you *can* meet your commitments one step at a time.

Celebrations don't have to be grand. It could be a simple self-high-five, a brief journal entry praising your efforts, or a playful sticker on your calendar to mark a completed task.

What matters is acknowledging your progress. Over time, these small affirmations add up, increasing your motivation and reducing your reliance on external validation.

You realize you can show up for yourself and reap the rewards of consistency.

Healthy Self-Talk

Accountability thrives when nurtured by **healthy self-talk**.

Replace phrases like "I messed up; I'm hopeless" with "I hit a snag today, but I can learn from it."

If you slip up—maybe you missed a deadline or procrastinated—try investigating the *why* without judgment. Were you overwhelmed? Did you need more clarity or resources?

Use the situation as a clue for improvement, not an opportunity to berate yourself. In essence, gentle accountability is a practice of curiosity, not condemnation.

The Role of Reflection

We touched on reflection in the time management segment, but it's equally essential for accountability. Weekly or bi-weekly, set aside 15–20 minutes to review your goals:

1. **What did I achieve that I'm proud of?**
2. **What barriers did I face, and how did I handle them?**
3. **Is there anything I need to change about my plan or approach?**
4. **Am I still enjoying the process, or am I feeling forced?**

This check-in anchors you to your "why"—the deeper reason you set these goals in the first place (maybe it's to live a less cluttered life, start a passion project, or cultivate healthier habits).

It also illuminates where you might need extra support or a tweak in strategy. The more you refine your approach, the more your confidence grows, creating a positive feedback loop that keeps you going.

Accountability Tools

In our digital age, there's no shortage of apps and platforms designed to help you track tasks and habits.

Trello, Asana, Habitica, or a simple Google spreadsheet can be external placeholders for your goals and progress.

Some people thrive on the gamification aspect, enjoying the sense of leveling up each time they complete a milestone.

Others find it more comforting to maintain a physical planner or bullet journal—something tangible you can hold.

Experiment to see what resonates. Remember that tools are only as good as your commitment to using them.

If you find an app draining or complicated, it may not fit.

Gentle accountability means choosing methods that reduce friction, not add to it.

A Quick Exercise: The Compassionate Check-In

Next time you fall short of a goal, try this:

1. **Pause** and take a deep breath.
2. **Name the Emotion**: Are you disappointed? Frustrated? Anxious?
3. **Identify the Cause**: Was the goal too big, the day too chaotic, or your energy too low?
4. **Offer Self-Kindness**: Remind yourself that slip-ups happen. "It's okay. One off-day doesn't define my entire effort."
5. **Revise the Plan**: If needed, adjust your goal or timeline.

These five steps transform a moment of "failure" into a stepping stone for learning, forging emotional resilience.

CONCLUSION TO CHAPTER 9

Productive Without the Pressure may sound like a paradox in a culture that equates frantic busyness with success.

But as we've uncovered in these pages, genuine productivity thrives on calm, intention, and self-compassion, not on driving yourself to the brink of burnout.

We began with **Time Management Basics**, discovering how prioritization, time blocking, and mindful end-of-day reviews can structure your day without chaining you to a rigid schedule.

The goal is to direct your energies more consciously, emphasizing the tasks that genuinely matter instead of scattering your focus on trivial pursuits.

Then, in **Focus and Flow**, we dipped into the art of deep engagement, where time melts away, creativity soars and productivity feels almost effortless.

By taming distractions, selecting appropriately challenging tasks, and perhaps even embracing rituals, we open the door to those elusive "flow states" that make work—and life—feel richer.

Finally, we explored **Gentle Accountability**, a counterpoint to the harsh self-criticism we know all too well. Whether leaning on a buddy system, setting S.M.A.R.T. goals, or celebrating small wins, gentle accountability holds us to our standards without dragging us through the mud when things go sideways.

Because life is messy, it's full of curveballs—some thrilling, some disheartening. Learning to adapt our goals and expectations with kindness keeps us in the game.

Imagine how your day-to-day would look if you consistently practiced these principles: less chaos, more clarity, less guilt, and more genuine progress.

You may be able to clock out of work (physical or mental) at a reasonable hour, enjoy hobbies or family time, and actually feel recharged enough to tackle tomorrow's tasks with optimism.

That's the essence of being "productive without the pressure."

Of course, it's a journey, not a final destination.

You'll have days where all these strategies go out the window—maybe you had a bad night's sleep or a last-minute crisis at work.

The objective measure of success isn't in never stumbling; it's in how quickly you dust yourself off and return to your mindful approach.

A single off day (or week or month) doesn't negate the benefits of your practice. Stay flexible, stay curious, and, above all, stay compassionate toward yourself.

You can redefine what "productive" means in your life. Is it about cramming every waking moment with busy work?

Or is it about moving purposefully, with clarity and joy, toward goals that resonate with your values?

That's your call to make. And if you ask me, the second option sounds much more appealing—and infinitely more sustainable.

So, take a moment now to reflect on what resonated most. It could be scheduling your day in blocks or trying out the Pomodoro Technique.

It could be creating a mini ritual to invite flow or starting a buddy system to keep you gently accountable.

Whatever you decide, remember that the ultimate aim is to relieve stress and live more fully, authentically, and with more appreciation for each small victory along the way.

May these insights guide you toward a more balanced, harmonious path of getting things done, one mindful step at a time.

CHAPTER 10
CULTIVATING SELF-COMPASSION

INTRODUCTION

Imagine for a moment that you're sitting in a cozy café, catching up with a friend going through a rough patch.

Maybe they messed up at work or argued with a loved one.

As they pour out their worries, you instinctively do your best to reassure them.

You tell them they're worthy, that one mistake doesn't define who they are, and that it's okay not to have everything figured out immediately.

You speak warmly and kindly—like a supportive beacon guiding them through the fog. Now, consider how you talk to yourself in similar moments of stress or disappointment.

Is that same gentle, understanding tone there, or do you catch yourself firing off harsh critiques, calling yourself names, and spiraling into guilt or shame?

Self-compassion is about learning to treat ourselves with the same care and understanding we'd offer a close friend.

It's the antidote to that inner critic who loves to point out every flaw, magnify every slip, and replay every embarrassing moment on a mental loop.

Here's the truth: beating ourselves up rarely leads to positive change. In fact, it often drags us into deeper pits of anxiety or despair.

When we cultivate self-compassion, we engage in **positive self-talk** (Subchapter 10.1), we learn to **forgive our past** blunders (Subchapter 10.2), and we discover how to **celebrate the small wins** that often go unnoticed (Subchapter 10.3).

These three elements form a powerful recipe for a more peaceful, resilient, and joyful life.

Why devote an entire chapter to self-compassion? Because it's the linchpin of emotional well-being.

Without it, the techniques you've learned in previous chapters—like mindfulness, boundary-setting, healthier habits, or stress management—might not stick.

You can have the world's best time-management system, but if your inner voice tears you down every time you slip, sustainable growth becomes a struggle.

Or you might adopt a fantastic exercise routine to sabotage yourself with harsh judgments the minute you skip a workout.

Self-compassion doesn't just help you handle stressful moments better; it reconfigures your internal narrative so you have the patience and kindness to keep going even when life throws a curveball.

Throughout this chapter, you'll explore concrete ways to shift your self-talk from critical to caring, come to terms with the parts of your past that still sting, and make a habit of noticing and celebrating your day-to-day achievements—even if they seem small at first glance.

We'll talk about the complexities, uncertainties, and nuances because no single approach works for everyone.

Think of this as an invitation to experiment, tweak, and discover how self-compassion feels in the unique landscape of your life.

One more note: self-compassion is not self-indulgence. It's not about letting yourself off the hook from responsibilities or ignoring areas where you want to grow.

It's about recognizing that growth is a journey and that mistakes are part of being human.

When you approach your challenges with gentleness, you free up emotional energy to address them rather than exhausting yourself with blame or shame.

Ready to see how this shift can lighten your load and help you stress less, live more, and feel genuinely at peace with yourself? Let's dive in.

10.1 POSITIVE SELF-TALK

The Voices in Our Heads

What would you hear if you stopped for a second and tuned into your internal monologue? Perhaps a litany of things you "should" do, scoldings for tasks left undone, or disparaging remarks about your body, personality, or abilities.

It's a sobering thought that, for many of us, the commentary inside our heads can be far more damaging than anything we'd dare say aloud to another person.

Here's the kicker: those internal words shape our feelings about ourselves and the world. They influence our emotional reactions, our decision-making, and even our resilience in the face of adversity.

The good news is we're not stuck with them. **Positive self-talk** is a skill that can be cultivated, fine-tuned, and strengthened—much like learning a musical instrument or a new language.

With consistent practice, you can transform the tenor of your inner voice from a harsh critic to a supportive ally.

Why Negative Self-Talk Feels So Automatic

Why is it easier to believe the critical voice than the kind one?

Our brain's **negativity bias** is a significant factor, an evolutionary quirk designed to help our ancestors survive.

The idea is simple: if our forebears remembered every potential threat—real or imagined—they were less likely to become a predator's lunch.

Fast-forward to modern life and that same bias can mean we dwell on mistakes and gloss over successes.

It's not because we're masochists; it's because our brains are wired to highlight anything that could go wrong.

Additionally, we might have picked up negative self-talk patterns from our upbringing or past experiences—maybe a teacher's harsh words or a parent's critical tone.

Once internalized, these tapes can replay in our minds for years, making them feel "normal."

Recognizing their origins can help us see that they're not necessarily accurate—they're just old scripts needing revision.

Reframing Your Inner Dialogue

So, how do you practice **positive self-talk** without feeling fake or Pollyannaish?

It helps to start with a technique called **cognitive reframing**. Instead of trying to force "happy thoughts" when you're feeling terrible, you look for a more balanced perspective.

Let's say you made a mistake at work. Your automatic thought might be, "I'm such an idiot. I can't do anything right."

A reframed thought could be, "I messed up that report, which isn't great.

But I can learn from it, fix what went wrong, and remember that I'm usually competent."

Notice how the second statement doesn't ignore the error—it acknowledges it but offers a kinder, more accurate view.

You still accept responsibility but refuse to equate one mistake with complete incompetence.

Over time, reframing teaches your brain to adopt a more supportive stance.

When a negative thought arises, you can ask:
1. **Is this thought 100% true?** More often than not, the answer is no.
2. **What evidence do I have that contradicts this?** This question prompts you to remember the times you succeeded.
3. **How would I phrase this if I were talking to a friend?** This is golden because it snaps you out of your harshness and helps you adopt a compassionate tone.

Mantras and Affirmations

People sometimes roll their eyes at **affirmations**, dismissing them as "woo-woo" or new-age. But when done right, they can be a potent tool for rewiring your internal monologue.

The key is to choose affirmations that resonate and don't feel absurdly out of reach.

For example, telling yourself, "I am a perfect human being who never makes mistakes," will likely trigger a skeptical laugh from your brain.

Instead, opt for something like, "I am learning and growing, and I'm allowed to make mistakes along the way."

You can write these affirmations on sticky notes, store them in a notes app on your phone, or even record voice memos.

The idea is to regularly expose yourself to these positive statements so they become part of your mental repertoire.

Think of affirmations as gentle reminders that challenge your negative beliefs head-on.

Self-Compassion Breaks

When you find yourself spiraling into self-criticism—maybe after a difficult conversation or a blunder—try taking a **self-compassion break.**

It can be as simple as:

- **Pause**: Close your eyes and take a deep breath.
- **Acknowledge**: Identify what you're feeling—hurt, embarrassment, frustration.
- **Remind Yourself You're Human**: Mistakes and imperfections are universal.
- **Offer Kindness**: Use phrases like, "May I be kind to myself in this moment" or "It's okay to feel how I'm feeling."

This mini-practice can shift you from panic or self-loathing into a more nurturing mind.

It might initially feel strange or awkward, but with repetition, it becomes a comforting ritual.

A Quick Exercise: The Thought-Tracking Journal

Take a week to keep a small journal (digital or paper) where you note down instances of negative self-talk.

When you catch a thought like, "I'm so lazy" or "I'll never get this right," jot it down. Then, next to it, write a reframed version.

Be honest, and don't try to sugarcoat everything. Just aim for a perspective that is factual and compassionate. After a few days, review your entries.

You'll likely spot patterns (like specific triggers or times of day) and may see a gradual shift in how you talk to yourself.

Positive self-talk is the bedrock of self-compassion, but it's not a standalone magic trick.

Often, we find it challenging to be kind to ourselves because we're dragging unresolved guilt or regrets.

That's where **forgiving your past** becomes essential.

Let's turn to Subchapter 10.2 to explore this often tricky but transformative process.

10.2 FORGIVING YOUR PAST

The Weight of Unresolved Regret

Ever feel like you're lugging around a heavy backpack stuffed with every mistake or regret you've accumulated over the years?

Maybe a moment from your teenage years still makes you cringe or a relationship choice you wish you could rewind.

Guilt and shame can cling to us like stubborn burrs, pricking us whenever we try to move forward.

This emotional baggage doesn't just weigh us down; it colors how we see ourselves in the present, feeding into negative self-talk and, by extension, heightened stress.

Forgiving your past is about **releasing** what no longer serves you.

That doesn't mean erasing memory or condoning harmful actions. It means acknowledging that you're no longer the person who made those choices, that you've evolved, and that continuing to punish yourself doesn't help anyone.

It's an act of emotional liberation, creating space for self-compassion to grow.

Myths About Forgiving Yourself

We resist self-forgiveness because we fear it lets us off the hook too quickly. *"If I forgive myself, won't I repeat the same mistakes?"* But genuine forgiveness doesn't mean shirking responsibility.

In fact, it often involves a deeper understanding of how and why you did what you did, which can prevent future slip-ups more effectively than self-condemnation ever could.

Another common myth is that self-forgiveness minimizes the impact of our actions on others. On the contrary, taking responsibility for the harm you caused—and, if possible, making amends—is often part of the forgiveness journey.

You're not pretending the event didn't happen, but recognizing continued shame or guilt doesn't rewrite the past. It only locks you in a mental prison.

Steps to Forgive Yourself

So, how do you begin this process? **Awareness** is the first step. Identify what precisely you haven't forgiven. Is it a single mistake or a pattern of behavior? Write it down if that helps.

Next, consider the circumstances at the time—the stressors, your emotional state, or any limiting beliefs. Understanding the "why" doesn't excuse the mistake but can foster empathy toward your younger or less-informed self.

- **Acknowledge the Harm**: Reflect honestly on whom your actions affected, including yourself. This step ensures you're not glossing over the issue.

- **Make Amends if Possible**: If you owe someone an apology, offering it can heal both sides. But do so without attaching strings or expectations of immediate forgiveness from them.

- **Embrace Self-Compassion**: Remind yourself that mistakes are part of being human. Think about what you learned from the experience.

- **Visualize Letting Go**: Some people find it helpful to imagine dropping a heavy weight or watching a written regret go up in flames (safely, of course). Symbolic gestures can reinforce the emotional release.

When Forgiveness is Complex

Some situations—like deeply traumatic events—can make self-forgiveness more complicated. Suppose you grew up in an abusive environment, for example.

In that case, you might blame yourself for not escaping sooner or how you coped.

In these cases, professional support (a therapist, counselor, or support group) might be crucial for navigating layers of pain and responsibility.

Healing isn't always linear, and there's no shame in seeking expert help.

Forgiveness vs. Amnesia

It's worth noting that forgiving your past doesn't mean forgetting it entirely.

Specific lessons or scars may remain, guiding you toward better decisions or reminding you of your strengths.

The goal is to find peace in the present, not to pretend the past never happened.

You can acknowledge those memories without letting them define or sabotage your happiness.

A Quick Exercise: The Forgiveness Letter

Consider writing a **forgiveness letter** to yourself. In this letter:

- **Describe What Happened**: Outline the event or pattern you struggle to forgive.
- **Acknowledge Emotions**: Let your feelings flow—anger, sadness, regret, confusion.
- **Offer Understanding**: Imagine you're writing to a friend who went through this. Offer empathy for the circumstances.
- **State Your Intention to Forgive**: You might write, "I forgive you, and I free you from the bonds of past mistakes. We are moving forward together."

You can keep this letter safe, tear it up afterward, or revisit it on tough days.

Putting your intention into words can be profoundly cathartic, shifting your self-talk away from blame and into compassion.

Once you've begun loosening the chains of old regrets, you open up mental and emotional real estate for more uplifting, affirming experiences.

And that's where **celebrating small wins** becomes transformative.

Let's explore that next in Subchapter 10.3.

10.3 CELEBRATING SMALL WINS

Why Little Victories Matter

Take a moment to think about how most of us approach goals.

We set a significant, shiny objective—like losing 20 pounds, landing a dream job, or writing a novel—and focus all our attention on that final result.

While having an end target is excellent, it can also overshadow the incremental steps and daily efforts that pave the way to success.

We forget that **progress** is rarely linear and that each small milestone deserves recognition.

You rob yourself of motivation and joy when you consistently overlook small wins. You might feel like you haven't achieved *anything* if you haven't hit the grand finale yet.

That sense of "I'm not there yet" can lead to stress, self-doubt, and even burnout.

Conversely, celebrating small wins recharges your emotional batteries, helps you track progress more accurately, and affirms that you're on the right path—even if you're not at the finish line.

The Science of Celebration

There's a psychological basis for why celebrating small milestones works.

Each time you acknowledge an accomplishment—no matter how minor—your brain releases **dopamine**, a neurotransmitter associated with pleasure and reward.

This dopamine hit functions like a mental "thumbs-up," encouraging you to repeat the behavior that led to the win.

Over time, celebration becomes more than just a feel-good activity; it's a strategic tool for building and sustaining healthy habits.

Moreover, celebrating successes counters the negativity bias we discussed earlier. It teaches your brain to notice what's going *right*, balancing out the habit of dwelling on mistakes or failures.

This is especially crucial if you're prone to self-criticism. Each small win you celebrate is another anchor pulling you toward a more positive self-view.

What Counts as a "Small Win"?

In a word, **anything**. Did you complete a workout when you almost skipped it? That's a win.

Did you speak up in a meeting when you'd typically stay quiet? Win.

Did you cook a healthy dinner instead of ordering fast food? Another win.

You may have recognized a negative thought and consciously chose to reframe it. Win again.

The point is that there's no universal scoreboard for small wins. It's all relative to your personal context and goals.

Something huge for you might be trivial for someone else, and vice versa.

The key is to tune in to your own journey and celebrate each step that moves you forward—no matter how tiny it seems from the outside.

Different Ways to Celebrate

The celebration doesn't have to mean throwing a party or breaking out the champagne (although you indeed can if the occasion calls for it!).

Often, the most effective forms of celebration are simple, consistent gestures that remind you to appreciate your growth:

- **Visual Trackers**: Consider a habit tracker or progress chart if you're a visual person. Each time you complete a small step—like writing 500 words or meditating for 10 minutes—check it off. Watching those checks accumulate can be surprisingly motivating.

- **Verbal Affirmations**: Pause and say out loud, "I did it! Good job, me." It might feel cheesy, but spoken words carry weight.

- **Share the News**: Text a supportive friend or post a quick update in a group chat. Sometimes, hearing someone else say, "That's awesome!" amplifies your own sense of pride.

- **Mini-Rewards**: Treat yourself to something you enjoy—maybe a 15-minute break to read a favorite book, a special snack, or time to play your favorite video game. Just be mindful if you have a history of emotional eating or spending; choose rewards that align with your well-being.

- **Reflect in a Journal**: Dedicate a page to "Today's Wins." Record moments of pride or achievement—even the seemingly ordinary ones. In time, these entries meld into an intricate mosaic that celebrates every small victory.

Turning Setbacks into Teachable Moments

Celebrating wins doesn't mean ignoring slip-ups. You'll still face setbacks or days that feel like total flops.

But with a celebratory mindset, those low points become learning opportunities.

Instead of labeling a tough day as a "failure," you can ask: *"Is there anything I can celebrate here?"*

You learned a crucial lesson about time management. You may have handled a conflict more calmly than a year ago.

Even amid struggle, there are often threads of progress if you know where to look.

Long-Term Impact of Celebrations

By regularly honoring your small wins, you cultivate a **growth mindset** that sees abilities as malleable and challenges as chances to improve.

You internalize the belief, *"I'm capable of progress, and it's happening all the time, even if I don't see huge leaps."*

This outlook can drastically reduce stress by encouraging patience and optimism rather than frantic pressure to achieve everything at once.

Moreover, celebrating small wins weaves with **positive self-talk** and **forgiving your past**. When you applaud what you're doing well, speaking kindly to yourself is easier.

When you let go of old regrets, you free up emotional space to focus on the accomplishments of the present moment.

All these components reinforce each other, creating a virtuous cycle of self-compassion and resilience.

A Quick Exercise: The Daily "High-Five"

Before you go to bed each night, give yourself a "high-five" for one thing you did well that day—no matter how trivial.

Maybe you drank an extra glass of water or finally cleared out an email backlog.

Acknowledge it, feel good about it, and then drift off to sleep with that positive note in mind.

You'll wake up more motivated than if you'd spent the night criticizing yourself for not doing more.

CONCLUSION TO CHAPTER 10

When was the last time you paused to extend empathy toward yourself—to really **feel** the weight you carry and think, *"I'm doing my best, and I deserve kindness too"*?

Cultivating self-compassion is a radical act in a culture that often equates self-worth with relentless productivity or external validation.

It's reclaiming your emotional well-being from the clutches of doubt, perfectionism, and criticism.

In **Positive Self-Talk**, we explored how to shift your internal script, recognizing that the voice inside your head can tear you down or lift you up.

By reframing negative thoughts, trying out affirmations, and allowing yourself mini-breaks of self-kindness, you dismantle the harsh narratives that keep you stuck.

Then, in **Forgiving Your Past**, we face the brutal reality that regrets and guilt can linger long after the event that caused them is over.

Self-forgiveness isn't about pretending mistakes didn't happen; it's about acknowledging them, learning from them, and releasing the perpetual self-punishment.

It's granting your past self the grace you wish someone had offered you sooner—thereby granting your present self the freedom to move forward without dragging old chains.

Finally, in **Celebrating Small Wins**, we discovered the importance of noticing the incremental victories that often go overlooked in our dash to the finish line.

Each time you honor a small achievement—sticking to a new habit for a day, showing courage in a conversation, or resisting an old, unhelpful urge—you teach your brain to focus on what's going right.

This boosts motivation and weaves a more optimistic narrative about who you are and what you can accomplish.

Together, these three components—*positive self-talk, forgiving your past,* and *celebrating small wins*—form a powerful cycle of self-compassion.

When you're gentler to yourself, you're more likely to see your mistakes as lessons, achievements as stepping stones, and daily life as an ongoing journey rather than a daunting final exam.

You reduce stress because you're no longer locked in a perpetual battle with your self-worth. You live more because you're free to savor each moment, unburdened by the fear of failing some invisible test.

Of course, self-compassion isn't a button you press once to magically transform your inner landscape.

It's more like learning a new language.

At first, you might stumble over unfamiliar phrases, revert to old habits, or even feel awkward speaking kindly to yourself. But the more you practice, the more fluent you become

Gradually, you'll notice that your default response to setbacks shifts from *"I'm terrible"* to *"I'm learning, and that's okay."*

You'll catch yourself celebrating little moments of progress, feeling a genuine warmth toward the person you see in the mirror.

What does this mean in the ***Stress Less, Live More*** scheme? It means you're giving yourself the emotional foundation to survive and thrive.

When life inevitably throws challenges your way, self-compassion acts like an emotional cushion.

You bounce back more quickly, with less self-inflicted misery.

You also find it easier to connect with others because you're not bogged down by the shame or negativity that once clouded your days.

Essentially, you become the sort of friend to yourself that you've always wanted—a supportive presence that sees your worth, no matter what.

So here's your invitation: Experiment with one practice from each subchapter over the next week.

Maybe you try reframing negative thoughts once daily, write a forgiveness letter to yourself about a lingering regret, and end each night with a quick high-five for something you did well.

Notice how these small shifts affect your mood, stress levels, and relationships.

Pay attention to any internal resistance, too—sometimes, the hardest part is simply letting go of the comfort we find in old patterns of self-criticism.

But keep going. Self-compassion is a gentle revolution, and every step you take is a testament to your willingness to be kind, honest, and grow.

Remember, cultivating self-compassion doesn't mean you'll never criticize yourself or feel regret again.

It means that when those feelings arise, you'll have the tools to address them constructively rather than letting them define you.

And that, in the dance of living, can make all the difference between constantly stumbling and learning to move with grace.

Here's to speaking kinder words inside our own heads, to making peace with the chapters of our past that still ache, and toasting every little spark of progress along the way.

Here's to a life where **stressing less** and **living more** become not just a mantra but a daily, compassionate reality.

CHAPTER 11
BUILDING INNER ENERGY

INTRODUCTION

Take a moment and imagine you're at the beginning of a long hike—maybe you're heading up a lush mountain trail or a winding forest path.

You've got a sturdy backpack, water, snacks, and the excitement of exploring somewhere new. But here's the catch: if you haven't slept well, if you haven't fueled your body correctly, or if your mind is weighed down by nonstop worries, that hike will feel twice as hard.

You might start with enthusiasm, but before long, your legs feel like lead, and you're questioning why you decided to climb a mountain in the first place.

Life can feel like that hike. When your energy reserves are low—emotionally, mentally, and physically—everything feels more difficult.

Work tasks, relationship challenges, personal goals... all these demands gnaw away at you, leaving you in a perpetual state of "just barely hanging on." That's not how you want to live.

Nor do you have to.

In this chapter, we'll explore how to **Build Inner Energy** so that you can tackle daily tasks, personal aspirations, and unexpected curveballs with a sense of vitality rather than exhaustion.

We'll start with **Finding Your Fuel** (Subchapter 11.1) because understanding what truly energizes you is like discovering the secret ingredient that makes you feel alive.

Next, we'll delve into **Protecting Your Vibe** (Subchapter 11.2), focusing on guarding your energy from draining influences—people, environments, or habits.

Finally, we'll reveal strategies for **Recharging for Growth** (Subchapter 11.3), ensuring that your newly cultivated energy doesn't burn out but propels you forward into a more expansive, joyful way of living.

Why is this so important? Because stress is sneaky. It drains you subtly until one day, you wake up feeling a shell of your former self—impatient, hopeless, or perpetually on edge.

By prioritizing your energy now, you shield yourself against this slow leak. You give yourself the bandwidth to engage with life wholeheartedly, whether pursuing a creative project, being present for loved ones, or simply relishing a peaceful morning cup of coffee.

And crucially, you learn that your energy isn't a fixed resource but something you can tend to and expand with deliberate care.

Picture each subchapter as a stepping stone across a stream of fatigue and overwhelm, guiding you to the other side where clarity, resilience, and excitement reside.

So, let's step onto the first stone and find out what truly fuels you.

11.1 FINDING YOUR FUEL

What Lights You Up?

Think about a moment when you felt genuinely alive—when time flew by effortlessly, and you were fully engaged in what you were doing.

Maybe it was during a creative endeavor like painting or writing, or you were engrossed in a fascinating conversation that left you buzzing with new ideas.

These moments aren't just happy accidents; they're breadcrumbs to understanding what fuels you at a deeper level.

Have you ever considered that what energizes one person might exhaust another? Some people thrive on social interactions—going to a party or a networking event can leave them glowing for hours.

Others find their energy in solitude, relishing a quiet evening with a good book.

Neither is inherently better; they're just different. The key is to identify the activities, environments, and passions that make *you* feel more vibrant, more "yourself," and more at peace.

Identifying Your Personal "Energy Pockets"

Sometimes, the best way to determine what fuels you is to look for "energy pockets." These are the parts of your life where you consistently leave feeling better than when you arrived.

Maybe it's:

- **A weekly yoga class** where you get an endorphin rush and a calmer mind.
- **That friend** who inspires you and fills conversations with laughter and warmth.
- **Gardening** on Saturday mornings, feeling the earth in your hands, and seeing life bloom under your care.
- **Reading fantasy novels** that transport you to magical worlds giving your imagination free rein.

Keep a small journal or note on your phone, documenting each time you feel a surge of positive energy.

Notice who you're with, what you're doing, and even the time of day.

After a week or two, patterns may emerge, pointing you toward your unique fuel sources.

Once identified, you can be more intentional about incorporating them into your routine.

The Power of Joyful Hobbies

Many adults complain that they no longer have hobbies, as though hobbies are a relic of childhood. But in truth, hobbies can be a wellspring of energy.

Remember that sense of glee you got as a kid while drawing, rollerblading, or collecting stickers? That joy is still inside you, waiting for an outlet.

When we label something "just a hobby," we often undervalue how much positive energy it can bring to our lives.

- **Creative Outlets**: Painting, crafting, cooking a new recipe—anything that lets you produce or explore can rekindle your spark.
- **Physical Pastimes**: Dancing, rock climbing, hiking—activities that engage your body, release endorphins, and counteract stress.
- **Mental Pursuits**: Learning a new language, tackling a challenging puzzle, or diving into a compelling podcast can fuel your mind.

Whatever your hobbies, give yourself permission to indulge in them regularly. Carving out even 15 minutes a day to do something that genuinely lights you up can shift your entire mood—and that sense of fulfillment can last longer than you might expect.

Balancing Challenge and Comfort

Some of your most energizing experiences involve a certain level of challenge. Perhaps it's finishing a tough workout or finally perfecting a piece of music on the piano.

Why does this feel so good? Because conquering a challenge sparks a rush of achievement and self-efficacy, a feeling of "I did it!"

But be mindful: too much challenge can lead to burnout; too little leads to boredom.

Ideally, you want to hover in that sweet spot where tasks are stimulating without being overwhelming—a zone psychologists often refer to as "flow."

Fuel vs. Distractions

Not every pleasurable activity is truly fueling. Sometimes, we conflate quick-fix distractions with genuine energy boosters.

Think about scrolling through social media for an hour. It might feel relaxing initially, but often, we emerge drained or vaguely uneasy.

Or consider binge-watching a show until 2 a.m.—it's entertaining at the time, but it robs you of sleep, leaving you groggy the next day.

Try to differentiate between **fuel** (activities that leave you feeling better in the long run) and **depleting distractions** (those that offer a short-term escape but ultimately drain your energy).

There's nothing wrong with enjoying a little mindless TV or social media, but be aware of when you cross from rejuvenation into self-sabotage.

A Quick Exercise: The "Energy Audit"

1. **List Your Daily Activities**: Jot down everything you typically do in a day—work tasks, household chores, leisure pursuits, etc.
2. **Rate the Energy Impact**: Next to each, mark whether it usually leaves you feeling energized (+), neutral (=), or drained (-).
3. **Identify Patterns**: Do you see clusters of pluses or minuses at certain times of day? Specific tasks that consistently light you up or bring you down?
4. **Make One Change**: Choose a draining activity you can modify or replace with something that gives you a boost.

For example, you could skip 15 minutes of social media doom-scrolling in favor of a quick walk outside.

By consciously seeking out and reinforcing your unique energy sources, you begin to shore up your inner reserves. But fueling your tank is only half the battle.

To maintain that energy, you'll need to guard it from draining influences—a task we'll tackle in the next subchapter **Protecting Your Vibe**.

11.2 PROTECTING YOUR VIBE

When "Good Vibes Only" Isn't Enough

We've all seen the popular mantra "good vibes only" splashed across social media, T-shirts, or coffee mugs.

While it's a nice sentiment, it can sometimes downplay the complexities of real life, where negative or draining experiences are inevitable.

We can't simply click our heels and banish every source of stress or negativity.

However, we *can* be more discerning about what we let into our mental and emotional space, effectively **protecting our vibe** from unnecessary drains.

Identifying Energy Vampires

Energy vampires aren't mythical bloodsuckers; they're the people, habits, or circumstances that consistently leave you feeling deflated.

It could be a coworker who always complains, a social media feed brimming with toxic debates, or even an old habit of ruminating over worst-case scenarios.

While some drains are unavoidable—like a demanding job or a family situation—others are optional, and we might not even realize how much they're eroding our well-being.

- **People**: Do you have friends or acquaintances who never ask how you are, only talk about their problems, or belittle your ideas?
- **Environments**: Is there a cluttered, noisy workspace that drives you nuts? Do you spend excessive time in virtual spaces that make you anxious or angry?

- **Habits**: Are you doom-scrolling the news before bedtime, guaranteeing anxious dreams?

The first step is noticing these influences. The second step is deciding if you can reduce your exposure to them or shift the dynamic so it's less draining.

That might mean setting boundaries with a friend, decluttering your environment, or committing to a "digital detox" period each day.

Setting Healthy Boundaries

We discussed boundaries in a previous chapter, but let's reiterate their importance for protecting your vibe.

Imagine your energy as a garden. If you don't fence it off, weeds (in the form of negativity or demands) can creep in and strangle your plants.

Setting boundaries might mean saying "no" to stressful events, limiting phone calls with specific individuals, or politely declining to engage in perpetual gossip or complaint sessions.

Boundaries can feel awkward if you're used to people-pleasing or avoiding confrontation. But remember, a boundary isn't an attack on someone else; it's a shield for your well-being.

Over time, you'll likely find that upholding boundaries isn't just protective—it helps you be more authentically present when you engage because you're not silently seething or feeling depleted.

Cultivating Protective Habits

Just as you can adopt habits that energize you, you can cultivate routines that shield you from unnecessary negativity:

- **Morning Intention-Setting**: Before diving into emails or social media, take a few minutes to breathe, stretch, or sip your coffee mindfully. Give yourself a calm buffer at the start of the day.
- **Digital Hygiene**: Mute or unfollow accounts that stir up stress or comparison. Schedule times to check your phone rather than letting it yank your attention 24/7.
- **Mental "Cleanup"**: Try a quick reality check if you dwell on toxic thoughts. Ask, "Is this thought helpful? Is it fact or fear? How can I redirect?" This mini-mindfulness can break the cycle of rumination.

Tools for Emotional Shielding

Sometimes, life throws negativity at you out of nowhere—a rude driver on your commute, a social media argument that sucks you in, or a tense family dinner.

To navigate these situations, consider "emotional shielding" techniques.

For instance, imagine a calm, glowing barrier around yourself, protecting you from other people's anger or snide remarks.

Visualizing a protective bubble can help you remain composed, preventing you from absorbing negative vibe.

Knowing When to Seek Support

No one can maintain an unshakable vibe all the time. If you're surrounded by ongoing toxicity—say, in a workplace or a relationship—it might be time to seek outside support.

Talk to a friend, therapist, or mentor who can offer perspective and practical advice. Recognize that "protecting your vibe" might not always be a DIY project; sometimes, you need guidance or a safe space to process your feelings and decide your next steps.

A Quick Exercise: The "Vibe Checklist"

In the morning or at the end of the day, do a "vibe checklist" for any encounters or situations that left a mark on you—positive or negative:

1. **Write them down**: E.g., "Argued with my coworker," "Had a great chat with my sister," "Spent an hour doomscrolling."
2. **Rate the impact**: Did the interaction leave you feeling + (good), − (drained), or ± (mixed)?
3. **Reflect**: If it was draining, how can you minimize or handle it differently next time? If it was uplifting, how can you get more of that?

This simple habit raises awareness, helping you steer your life toward healthier vibes. Once you're fueling yourself effectively and shielding your vibe from undue negativity, the last piece of the puzzle is learning how to **recharge** to keep growing without burnout.

Let's explore that in the next subchapter.

11.3 RECHARGING FOR GROWTH

The Myth of Constant Hustle

We live in a hustle-obsessed culture that praises grinding until you drop. But when you're always "on," you never have a chance to refill your energy reservoir.

Eventually, the well runs dry, and you're left wondering why you feel so stressed and unfulfilled. *In reality, rest is not a luxury but a necessity.*

Like a smartphone needing periodic charging, you also require consistent downtime to operate at your best.

Embracing Cycles of Activity and Rest

Nature is cyclic—day turns to night, seasons shift, tides ebb and flow. Our bodies and minds also function best when given a natural rhythm of exertion and recovery.

After intense focus or physical effort, you need a period of rest. This could be a lunch break where you step away from your desk, an evening walk after a busy day, or a day off after a week of intense work.

Pushing through exhaustion might feel heroic in the moment, but it inevitably leads to diminishing returns.

Active Rest vs. Passive Rest

Not all rest is created equal. **Passive rest** involves activities like lying on the couch, watching TV, or scrolling on your phone, requiring minimal effort.

That can be okay in small doses, especially if you're physically worn out. However, **active rest**—such as gentle stretching, casual walks, or creative hobbies—often does more for recharging your mind and spirit.

These activities engage your body and senses without overwhelming them, helping you decompress and regain energy more holistically.

- **Mindful Breaks**: Even a simple three-minute breathing exercise can reset your nerves when frazzled. Close your eyes, inhale slowly, and exhale gently, feeling the tension drain with each breath.
- **Nature Therapy**: Spending time in green spaces has been shown to reduce stress hormones. Whether you prefer a scenic hike or a quick stroll in a local park, nature can recharge you in ways indoor activities often can't.
- **Play**: Tap into your inner child by playing board games with friends, dancing around your living room, or wrestling with your kids or pets. Play unlocks a carefree, joyful energy that adult life often stifles.

Scheduling Downtime to Grow

Sometimes, we imagine that growth and progress only happen when we're actively "doing" something—learning new skills, working on a project, networking.

But paradoxically, real insights often arise during downtime. *Ever notice how your best ideas pop up in the shower or on a relaxed weekend?* That's your brain capitalizing on a mental break, connecting dots that were previously scattered.

Schedule deliberate downtime if you want to accelerate your personal or professional development. This might mean:

- **Blocking off weekends** where you decline extra work or major social commitments.
- **Taking micro-retreats**—short vacations or day trips to explore a new place or immerse yourself in nature.
- **Implementing a Sabbath day** means unplugging electronics, errands, or chores for 24 hours.

Don't be surprised if you return from these breaks brimming with fresh perspectives and enthusiasm for your next steps.

Reflection for Sustainable Growth

Recharging isn't just about unplugging; it's also about **reflecting** on what's happened and where you want to go. After you've rested, carve out a few minutes—or an entire afternoon if you can—to think about:

1. **Recent Progress**: What milestones or achievements have you reached?
2. **Current Challenges**: Are there hurdles still wearing you down? How can you address them without depleting your energy?
3. **Future Vision**: What do you aspire to in the coming weeks, months, or years? Does your routine support that vision, or do you need adjustments?

This reflection ensures that when you jump back into action, you do so with clarity and renewed motivation rather than stumbling in the dark.

A Quick Exercise: The "Recharge Menu"

Create a personal "Recharge Menu" of activities that help you feel rested and revitalized.

It might look like this:

- **5-Minute Recharges**: Deep breathing, standing stretches, quick journaling, a glass of water.
- **30-Minute Recharges**: Walk around the block, read a chapter of a fun novel, play a short music playlist, and dance in your room.
- **1–2 Hour Recharges**: A relaxed coffee catch-up with a friend, cooking a healthy meal, or a restorative yoga class.
- **Weekend/Full-Day Recharges**: A nature hike, a day trip to a museum, a family barbecue where you set your phone aside.

Keep this menu somewhere accessible—your phone, a sticky note on your desk—and pull it out whenever you sense your energy running low.

That way, you're not fumbling for an idea now; you already have a trusted repertoire of stress-busting, spirit-lifting activities.

CONCLUSION TO CHAPTER 11

When we talk about **Building Inner Energy**, it's easy to think of it as a one-time fix—like filling up your gas tank and then driving until it's empty. But the reality is more dynamic.

Energy isn't just physical stamina; it's emotional resilience, mental clarity, and a sense of purpose that makes everyday challenges feel surmountable rather than soul-crushing.

By weaving together the principles from these three subchapters, you create a continuous cycle of energizing, safeguarding, and renewing yourself.

In **Finding Your Fuel**, we learned to identify what lights us up—those moments when we feel engaged, alive, and at peace.

Whether painting, dancing, solving puzzles, or having a deep conversation with a close friend, acknowledging what fuels you is half the battle.

Once you know, you can make more room for these energies, cultivating them like precious seedlings.

From there, **Protecting Your Vibe**, taught us to guard that energy from external drains—people, environments, and habits that siphon off our vitality.

Setting boundaries is crucial: it might mean limiting screen time or cutting back on social events that leave us depleted.

It might also mean practicing mental shielding techniques or gracefully diffusing conflict.

Each time you stand up for your peace, you reinforce that your well-being matters.

Finally, in **Recharging for Growth**, we saw that rest and reflection aren't luxuries but essential components of sustainable progress.

By embracing cyclic rhythms—work and rest, focus and play—we allow ourselves to bounce back stronger after each period of effort.

Whether it's a five-minute breather or a weekend retreat, these active rests refuel our body, mind, and spirit, helping us avoid the pitfall of chronic stress or burnout.

Think of this entire process like tending a fire. You gather the proper logs (the fuel that excites you), shield them from the wind (protecting your vibe), and occasionally let the flames rest or add kindling when necessary (recharging for growth).

With consistent care, your inner fire burns steady and bright, ready to warm you through life's winters and illuminate your path forward.

As you apply these principles, you may find that your newfound energy opens doors you hadn't considered—maybe you'll tackle a project you've been too tired to start or reconnect with friends and family in more meaningful ways.

Building inner energy isn't a one-time project; it's an ongoing dance of noticing when you're out of balance and then gently steering yourself back toward equilibrium.

Yes, there will be days or weeks when the dance feels clumsy—where unexpected crises or emotional hurdles leave you feeling depleted.

In those times, it's okay to slow down, focus on self-care, and remind yourself that energy can be replenished with mindful attention and kindness to your needs.

How might you take a first step right now? Maybe it's identifying one "energy pocket" activity you can do today or setting a boundary around a draining conversation you've been having too frequently.

Perhaps it's a commitment to a short walk in nature this weekend or a promise to turn off your phone an hour before bedtime for a more restful night.

Each small choice, each boundary set, and each moment of rest is a brick in the foundation of your well-being.

Because when you nurture your inner energy, you're not just surviving—you're thriving.

You're creating a life where stress is managed and challenges become opportunities for growth rather than triggers for meltdown.

And isn't that, in the end, the true essence of **Stress Less, Live More**? A life fueled by the things that matter to you, shielded from unnecessary drains, and continually recharged for the next adventure waiting around the corner.

CHAPTER 12
FINDING MOMENTS OF JOY

INTRODUCTION

Close your eyes for a moment—imagine a life where little pockets of delight appear throughout your day like hidden gems waiting to be discovered.

One minute, you're stuck in traffic or preparing your morning coffee, and the next minute, you notice a baby bird perched on a nearby tree branch, singing its tiny heart out.

You pause, smile, and—like that—you feel your heart lift. That's the power of a joyful moment.

Now, picture stitching these tiny, gleaming pearls of joy together, creating a chain that could light up even the dreariest of days.

You don't need a big promotion, a lavish vacation, or an extravagant party to feel good about life.

Sometimes, all it takes is stepping outside for a few minutes, tasting your favorite ice cream scoop, or even enjoying that first sip of tea in the morning.

And there's nothing trivial about these experiences: they recharge you, ground you, and remind you that life is more than just checking off to-do lists and worrying about the future.

In this chapter, we'll embark on a journey of **Finding Moments of Joy**—those brief yet potent windows that can turn an ordinary Tuesday into something magical.

We'll begin with **Mini-Break Adventures** (Subchapter 12.1), showing how mini-escapes peppered throughout your day or week can transform your relationship with stress.

Next, we'll dive into the habit of **Joy Journaling** (Subchapter 12.2). This daily practice helps you capture and reflect on those bright spots, no matter how fleeting they seem.

Finally, we'll unlock **The Power of Play** (Subchapter 12.3), proving that play isn't just for kids—it's a cornerstone of emotional resilience and creative living.

Don't worry; you won't have to overhaul your life or adopt complicated new systems.

The beauty of joy is that it often arises from small adjustments in perspective.

It's not about denying life's challenges—those are real and can be tricky.

Instead, it's about finding glimmers of light amidst the shadows, learning to dance in the rain, and permitting yourself to exhale, smile, and even laugh at the absurdity of it all.

Ready to shift your mindset and begin inserting more joy into your daily life?

Explore the first subchapter and discover how simple, bite-sized adventures can lift your spirits.

12.1 MINI-BREAK ADVENTURES

The Big Impact of Small Escapes

Picture this scenario: You're sitting at your desk, eyeing that never-ending list of tasks, feeling your stress level inching upward.

What if you could press a "pause" button on the rush and step away—even for only five minutes—to recharge yourself?

Sometimes, a **mini-break adventure** is precisely what you need to interrupt the hamster wheel of stress.

But wait, you might think, *"A mini-break? I barely have time to eat lunch!"* That's the beauty of these tiny escapes: they don't require large chunks of time or elaborate planning.

They're quick bursts of novelty, relaxation, or exploration that can fit seamlessly into your daily routine.

Whether it's a five-minute stroll around the block, a 15-minute detour to a local park, or even a 30-second meditation at your desk, each mini-break is a small act of reclaiming your well-being.

Escaping the Rut with Micro-Adventures

Ever notice how daily life can become so repetitive that days blur together like reruns of the same TV show?

That's where micro-adventures step in, injecting fresh energy into your routine without demanding a plane ticket or a cleared-out weekend. A micro-adventure could be:

- **Try a new walking path** during your lunch break.
- **Sampling a local café's pastry** you've never tasted before.

- **Listening to a five-minute travel vlog** that transports your mind across the globe.
- **Practicing a quick yoga flow** outside, feeling the sun on your skin.

These little detours break the monotony and spark curiosity. They remind you there's room for discovery even in a familiar environment if you look closely enough.

That spark of novelty is rejuvenating; it can elevate your mood and refuel your creativity for the tasks ahead.

Breaking the All-or-Nothing Mentality

One of the biggest barriers to finding joy in daily life is the belief that relaxation or adventure must be large-scale.

We wait for a dream vacation or a full weekend getaway before we "allow" ourselves to unwind. Yet, that approach can leave us constantly drained, trudging through the week without real respite.

Mini-break adventures challenge that mentality, offering a more sustainable way to manage stress. Instead of living for the two-week vacation you might take next year, you treat each day like a canvas where small bursts of enjoyment can be painted.

Crafting Your Mini-Break Menu

So how do you get started? Begin by brainstorming a "mini-break menu."

Think of easy, enjoyable actions that can be done in five to fifteen minutes—things that bring you a spark of delight or relaxation:

- **Nature Moments**: Step outside and watch the clouds, stand beneath a tree, or listen for birdsong.
- **Sensory Pleasures**: Brew a cup of fragrant herbal tea and sip it slowly, savoring the aroma. Or unroll a yoga mat for gentle stretches that awaken your body.
- **Quick Social Boosts**: Text a friend a funny meme, send a voice note of gratitude to someone who brightened your day, or strike up a friendly chat with a coworker.
- **Micro-Hobbies**: If you love doodling, set a timer and sketch for five minutes. Or learn a few phrases in a new language. Mini tasks stimulate your mind and break you out of the daily grind.

Pick an item from your mini-break menu when you notice your stress creeping up—maybe your shoulders are tense, or your patience is wearing thin.

Allow yourself that brief escape. You might be surprised how this small pivot can reset your mindset and boost your energy, enabling you to tackle your responsibilities with renewed clarity.

Overcoming Guilt

Some feel guilty about leaving work or chores for these little adventures. They think, *"Shouldn't I just power through?"*

But consider this: pushing through exhaustion or stress often results in diminished productivity and higher irritability.

A short break can be far more beneficial than an extra 15 minutes of forced labor. Plus, by weaving moments of joy into your day, you're effectively training your brain to recognize and appreciate life's simpler pleasures.

Your overall stress levels decrease, and your sense of presence increases.

A Quick Exercise: The Surprise Stroll

Next time you have an unscheduled five or ten minutes—maybe a meeting finishes early, or you arrive somewhere before your friend—go for a "surprise stroll."

No specific destination is required. Just walk around the block or down the hall, noticing your surroundings with fresh eyes.

Look for something interesting or beautiful you've never seen—a unique architectural detail, colorful flower, and funny bumper sticker.

Let this mini-break open your sense of wonder, reminding you that enjoyment isn't confined to special occasions.

Once you start sprinkling mini-break adventures throughout your routine, you'll find daily life feels less like a grind and more like a series of opportunities to reconnect with yourself and the world around you.

But these uplifting moments can sometimes slip through the cracks of our memory if we don't capture them.

That's where **Joy Journaling** comes in, our next topic.

12.2 JOY JOURNALING

Why Writing Down Joy Matters

Imagine you just had a brief yet wonderful experience—like catching a brilliant sunset or sharing a hearty laugh with a loved one. In the moment, it warms your heart.

But how often do these small joys fade away by the next day, overshadowed by urgent emails or lingering worries?

Joy journaling is a practice designed to keep those moments from slipping through the cracks of memory. By intentionally writing down episodes of joy, you anchor them in your consciousness.

This isn't about living in denial of problems; it's about balancing the scales and ensuring you're paying attention to what's beautiful, fun, or heartwarming in your world.

The Science of Gratitude and Positive Focus

You might wonder, *"Does writing a few lines each day really help me stress less?"* Research suggests that it does.

When people systematically note down positive experiences or things they're grateful for, they often report lower stress levels, increased optimism, and even improved physical health.

In a world dominated by negative headlines and personal responsibilities, consistently focusing on the good can shift your mental filters.

You begin to see opportunities for joy where you previously only saw obstacles.

What to Include in Your Joy Journal

A joy journal isn't meant to be an artistic masterpiece or a literary endeavor. It can be as straightforward as bullet points or short sentences capturing snippets of your day. Here's what you might include:

- **Small Wins**: Did you solve a tricky problem at work or finally tackle that cluttered corner of your living room?
- **Sensory Delights**: Maybe you inhaled the aroma of fresh bread while walking past a bakery or felt the soft warmth of your pet curled up beside you.
- **Kindness Received or Given**: A compliment from a friend, a favor you did for a neighbor or a sweet message from a loved one.
- **Moments of Laughter**: That hilarious meme someone sent you or a silly joke you overheard.
- **Nature's Gifts**: A glimmer of sunshine after a rainy day, the delicate petals of a flower, or the soothing sound of rain on your window.

Even if a day feels heavy, there's often at least one bright spot—like an unexpected text from a friend or the simple pleasure of a warm shower.

By consistently journaling these moments, you train your mind to be on the lookout for them in real-time.

Making It Manageable

One common hurdle is finding the time or discipline to keep a journal. To make it easier:

- **Keep It Short**: Just a few lines or bullet points are enough.
- **Choose a Consistent Time**: Some people like to journal in the morning to start their day on a positive note, while others prefer doing it at night to reflect before sleep.
- **Use Any Medium**: Whether it's a fancy notebook, a simple spiral-bound pad, a digital note-taking app, or even voice memos—pick what feels most natural.
- **Be Flexible**: Don't let guilt pile up if you miss a day or two. Just jump back in when you can.

The Emotional Safety Net

Over time, your joy journal can become a resource for tough days. Feeling down or stuck in a spiral of negative thoughts?

Flip back through old entries and relive memories of joy. This isn't just an exercise in nostalgia; it's a reminder that life isn't all gloom.

You've experienced bright, satisfying moments before and experience them again.

When Journaling Feels Forced

If you're going through a particularly rough patch, "joy journaling" might feel contrived. *"How can I write about good things when I'm upset or anxious?"* you might ask.

In those times, consider focusing on *tiny* joys—a good cup of coffee, the comfort of your bed, or the reliability of your favorite pen.

Don't pressure yourself to feel euphoric; just note the small consolations or mild pleasures. Even this gentle acknowledgment can help crack open the door for more positive feelings to seep in.

A Quick Exercise: The "3-2-1" Technique

Each evening, try noting:

- **3 small joys** from today (maybe the taste of a new snack, a kind email, a moment of peace).

- **2 ways you added to someone else's joy** (like sending a supportive message or offering help).

- **1 intention** for finding joy tomorrow (a mini goal: "I'll take a five-minute walk before lunch," or "I'll try that new chai latte flavor").

This structured approach guides you toward receiving and giving joy, nurturing a more balanced sense of well-being.

By journaling these little joys, you store them for future reflection and create a habit of noticing them in the first place.

It's like tuning your brain to a different radio frequency that regularly broadcasts small notes of happiness even amid the static of daily stress.

But there's another way to tap into joy that might bring a bigger smile to your face: **play**.

The following subchapter shows how childish fun can be a grown-up's secret weapon for resilience.

12.3 THE POWER OF PLAY

Rediscovering a Lost Art

Remember your delight as a child playing tag or building forts out of couch cushions? Back then, time felt infinite, and the primary goal was to have fun—no agenda, no guilt, just pure, unadulterated play.

Yet, as adults, we often push play to the sidelines, prioritizing productivity and responsibilities. Adult life requires us to juggle obligations, but must that mean we abandon play altogether?

Reintroducing **play** into our lives isn't about shirking duties; it's about reclaiming a source of creative energy, stress relief, and emotional renewal. When you give yourself permission to be playful—even for a few minutes—you can break the cycle of tension that weighs you down.

Suddenly, the world feels less ominous, your problems more solvable, and your spirit significantly lighter.

The Health Benefits of Play

The concept of adult play isn't just whimsical. It has real benefits:

- **Stress Reduction**: Laughter and carefree activity lower cortisol levels, helping you relax more deeply.
- **Creativity Boost**: Play expands your thinking, sparking new ideas and solutions you might not find through linear logic.
- **Social Connection**: Group play—like board games, group sports, or escape rooms—cultivates camaraderie and stronger bonds.

- **Mood Uplift**: Physical movement and friendly competition can release endorphins, those feel-good chemicals your body produces.

Plus, play helps you develop resilience. You learn to experiment, adapt, and not take failures too seriously.

After all, losing a game of charades is hardly the end of the world. Still, it might teach you about spontaneity, humor, and the joy of shared experiences.

Types of Play for Busy Adults

"Play" might sound vague or silly until you realize it can take many forms, from quiet and imaginative to active and competitive. Consider:

1. **Solo Play**: Puzzles, adult coloring books, doodling, or building something with your hands (like a Lego set or a DIY craft).
2. **Play with Friends or Family**: Board games, karaoke nights, spontaneous dance-offs, or a pick-up sports game at the park.
3. **Play with Strangers**: Joining a local improv class, a recreational sports league, or even an online gaming community can offer the novelty of connecting with new people.
4. **Digital Play**: Video games, virtual reality experiences, or playful apps that let you create music, art, or silly animations.

The key is to pick something that excites you or piques your curiosity. It doesn't have to be a massive time commitment—maybe 15 minutes of messing around with a creative app could be enough to brighten your day.

Navigating Adult Inhibitions

Many of us struggle with the idea of adult play because we worry about looking childish or irresponsible. We're conditioned to see grown-up life as serious, and our time is strictly devoted to "productive" endeavors.

But here's a reality check: being playful doesn't negate your maturity or responsibilities. It's an additional layer that makes you more versatile, adaptable, and happier.

If you feel self-conscious, start small. Try a playful activity in the privacy of your home—maybe an online dance tutorial or a funny voice-over app. Once you feel more comfortable, you can invite a friend or partner to join you.

Incorporating Play into Everyday Life

Rather than treating play as a separate event—like a monthly game night—why not sprinkle playful elements into your daily routine? Examples include:

- **Turning chores into a game**: Set a timer for 10 minutes and see how many clothes you can fold before the buzzer rings.
- **Race the clock**: Challenge yourself to tidy up your desk within a certain number of songs on your playlist.
- **Use playful language**: In your to-do app, rename your tasks with silly or imaginative titles. Instead of "Send weekly report," type "Unleash the data dragon." It

sounds goofy, but it can turn a mundane chore into something more playful.

By weaving play into ordinary tasks, you invite a sense of lightness that counters the oppressive feeling of endless adult responsibilities.

A Quick Exercise: The 5-Minute Playground

Set a timer for five minutes. In that short window, do something utterly playful:

- **Draw stick-figure comics** of your day's events.
- **Make funny faces** at yourself in the mirror.
- **Bounce a small ball** around your room, seeing how many times you can catch it in a row.
- **Hum a favorite tune** and make up silly lyrics on the spot.

It might feel ridiculous at first, but notice your mood afterward.

You'll experience a mini-surge of endorphins and a sense of liberation from your usual mental constraints.

CONCLUSION TO CHAPTER 12

And there you have it—a roadmap to **Finding Moments of Joy** in the swirl of modern life.

We began with **Mini-Break Adventures**, exploring how short bursts of escapism can bring immediate relief and a renewed spirit to your daily grind.

No plane tickets or massive chunks of free time are required—just the willingness to break your routine for a few minutes and savor something fresh.

Then, we discovered the art of **Joy Journaling**, a tangible way to capture those fleeting instances of happiness before they fade into oblivion.

This practice preserves your joyful memories and trains your brain to seek and relish the good.

Finally, we unleashed **The Power of Play**, reminding ourselves that grown-ups can—and should—rediscover a sense of wonder and lightheartedness. Play is mood-boosting.

Integrating these ideas into your daily routine may feel awkward initially, especially if you're used to taking life very seriously.

That's normal. Think of it this way: Joy, like any habit, takes practice. You're learning a new language that emphasizes humor, curiosity, and a willingness to let go of strict expectations.

Don't expect an overnight transformation; watch how these small efforts accumulate over weeks, gradually pulling you toward a lighter, more joyful outlook on life.

And yes, challenges will persist. Bills must still be paid, errands run, and problems solved.

But here's the shift: you build resilience when you continually invite joy into your day.

Stressful events no longer dominate your emotional landscape because you have a repertoire of quick, uplifting strategies.

You become someone who can navigate difficulties without losing sight of life's sweeter notes.

So what's your next step? Will you try a micro-adventure tomorrow—like taking a new route home or sampling a new fruit at the grocery store?

Or perhaps you'll start scribbling small joys in a pocket notebook tonight or challenge a friend to a silly game of charades this weekend.

Each of these moves, however small, contributes to a mosaic of a well-lived life marked not only by achievements but also by bursts of laughter, moments of awe, and a sense that every day holds at least a dash of magic.

Yes, it might feel like we're living in uncertain times, with more than enough reasons to worry.

But joy is still an option. In fact, it may be more necessary than ever. Joy, in its fleeting yet potent form, can ground us, heal us, and remind us of our shared humanity.

The next time you feel stress creeping into your bones, pause, take a breath, and remember: a mini-break adventure awaits, a joy journal is eager to capture your thoughts, and the spirit of play is always ready to welcome you back into its world of open-ended wonder.

CHAPTER 13
CONNECTING WITH OTHERS

INTRODUCTION

Take a moment and think about the last time someone genuinely supported you. Maybe it was a friend who showed up with coffee during a rough day or a coworker who offered to share the load on a big project.

Perhaps a family member was giving you a hug at just the right moment. There's a warmth in those connections that goes beyond polite niceties; it's a sense of belonging, of being seen and cared for.

Now, think about how your stress levels shift in those moments. Odds are, they go down. You feel lighter, safer, and more confident that you can tackle whatever challenge lies ahead.

That's the power of human connection.

Despite living in a world where we can text each other from across the globe in seconds, many of us still wrestle with loneliness, isolation, or the impression that our struggles are ours to bear alone.

But here's the wonderful thing: forming and maintaining supportive, empathetic relationships doesn't just help us survive—it helps us **thrive**.

This chapter, **"Connecting with Others,"** focuses on how robust relationships and social skills can be a secret weapon against stress, keeping us healthier, happier, and more resilient in life's ups and downs.

We'll start by examining **Support Networks** (Subchapter 13.1), exploring why no one is meant to go it alone and how we can create webs of connection that stand the test of time.

Then, we'll delve into **Practicing Empathy** (Subchapter 13.2), revealing how seeing the world through someone else's eyes can strengthen bonds, diffuse conflicts, and even reduce our anxiety.

Lastly, we'll round things out by discussing **Nurturing Your Relationships** (Subchapter 13.3) and sharing practical (and sometimes lighthearted) strategies to keep your connections strong and meaningful in a hectic world.

By the end of this chapter, I hope you'll feel more prepared to lean on and learn from those around you and more confident in your ability to offer that same compassion and care in return.

Because let's face it: we all need each other.

And in learning to rely on one another—even in the smallest of ways—we discover a powerful antidote to stress and a direct pathway to living more fully, joyfully, and authentically.

13.1 SUPPORT NETWORKS

Why We're Not Meant to Do This Alone

Raise your hand if you've ever prided yourself on being "independent."

Many of us grew up believing that asking for help is a sign of weakness, that we should handle our problems independently, or that self-sufficiency is the hallmark of success. But let's be honest: the human species has always thrived in groups.

Whether it's ancient tribes relying on collective hunting and shared child-rearing or modern coworkers collaborating on big projects, we've evolved to cooperate.

Studies consistently show that having a reliable social network contributes to everything from lower blood pressure to increased longevity.

It's not just about the occasional beer with friends or superficial water-cooler chats, though those can be pleasant.

It's about having a circle (or several circles) of people you can turn to when life gets messy.

This group celebrates your wins and offers a shoulder (or three) to cry on during the tough times.

Types of Support

Not all support is the same, and that's okay. Some folks are excellent at providing emotional comfort—listening empathetically, validating your feelings, or offering a warm hug when you're down.

Others might be your go-to for practical help: the coworker who's always ready to share resources, the neighbor with the perfect toolbox for your latest home project, or the friend who doesn't mind driving you to the airport at 5 a.m.

We also have different "zones" of connection:

1. **Inner Circle**: Call these folks at 2 a.m. in a crisis. Spouses, best friends, close family—people who see you at your most vulnerable and love you anyway.

2. **Middle Circle**: Good friends or coworkers you trust to some extent. They might not know your deepest secrets, but you can rely on them for help or a friendly ear.

3. **Outer Circle**: You see acquaintances, neighbors, or community members occasionally. They provide a sense of belonging but may not be intimately involved in your daily life.

Each circle has value. The idea is to ensure you have enough connection and variety in your support network to avoid placing all your emotional eggs in one fragile basket. It also means you can offer different kinds of support to others, depending on the closeness of your relationship and your personal strengths.

Building Your Village

Take heart if you're feeling a little isolated right now or your existing relationships have lost some spark.

Building or revitalizing a support network isn't rocket science but requires intentionality. Here are a few steps:

- **Identify Gaps**: Do you have many acquaintances but crave a more profound friendship? Or do you lack practical support, like someone to help with errands or pet-sitting? Write down what you're missing and set small goals to fill those gaps.

- **Join Groups**: Whether it's a volunteer organization, a book club, or a sports league, shared activities are a natural way to meet like-minded people. Connection often flows more easily when you bond over shared interests.
- **Reconnect with Old Friends**: Sometimes, the best connections are ones we've let slide. Send that message. Schedule that catch-up call. You might be surprised how quickly the old warmth returns.
- **Use Online Communities Wisely**: Digital spaces (like a parenting forum or a local community Facebook group) can be great for sharing tips or seeking help. However, they should complement in-person connections, not replace them entirely.

Remember, building a reliable support system takes time. Don't be discouraged if your first attempts at expanding your network don't lead to instant bosom buddies.

Trust that every effort, conversation, and new experience will help lay a foundation for more meaningful connections in the future.

Offering Support to Receive Support

Oddly enough, one of the most effective ways to cultivate a robust network is to practice generosity toward others.

When you try to help—whether it's offering a listening ear, a ride, or even a small favor—you build goodwill.

People sense your sincerity, and reciprocal warmth often follows. It doesn't mean you should give selflessly while expecting nothing in return.

A Quick Exercise: The Support Map

1. **Grab a piece of paper** and draw a circle in the center. Write "Me" inside it.
2. **Around that circle**, draw one ring for your inner circle, another for your middle circle, and an outer ring for acquaintances or the broader community.
3. **Place the names of people** in the appropriate rings, mapping out your current network. Don't forget online friends, coworkers, or extended family.
4. **Reflect**: Where do you see gaps? Maybe you're missing someone you can go to for career advice or feel your old friends live too far away. Identify at least one small step you can take—like rejoining a professional group or texting an old buddy—to strengthen that zone.

By understanding your existing network and the areas that need attention, you'll be better positioned to reduce feelings of isolation and stress.

Plus, you'll know exactly whom to reach out to in a pinch. Next, let's deepen our ability to connect by honing a crucial life skill: **Empathy**.

13.2 PRACTICING EMPATHY

What Is Empathy, Really?

If you've ever had a conversation with someone who truly "gets" you—who doesn't just nod politely but actually understands the heart of what you're saying—you've experienced Empathy.

Empathy is the capacity to sense and share another person's emotions, to slip into their perspective without losing your own.

It's different from sympathy, which often involves feeling sorry for someone. Empathy is more active and more relational. It's about resonating with another's emotional experience.

But let's be honest: Empathy isn't always easy. Our thoughts, judgments, and biases can block it. We might rush to offer advice or feel uncomfortable with someone else's pain.

We also worry that genuinely understanding another's sorrow or anger could weigh us down.

Yet Empathy is essential for forging deep, meaningful connections—the glue binds friendships, families, and communities together.

The Neuroscience of Empathy

Studies in social neuroscience show that specific brain circuits light up when we observe others in pain or hear them describe their struggles.

In a way, we simulate their experience in our own neural pathways. This is why you might physically cringe when someone tells a painful injury or tear up when you hear a moving story.

We're wired for Empathy, at least in potential. However, stress, time constraints, or personal issues can dampen this natural capacity.

The good news is that Empathy can be developed like a muscle. With deliberate practice, you can grow more skilled at tuning in to others.

As you do, you'll find that your relationships become stronger, conflicts resolve more easily, and ironically, your own stress may lessen.

When you understand someone else's perspective, you reduce the friction caused by misunderstandings and guesswork.

The Three Levels of Empathy

1. **Cognitive Empathy** is understanding someone's viewpoint or reasoning without getting emotionally involved. It's like saying, "I see why you think that."
2. **Emotional Empathy** involves feeling what the other person feels, such as sadness, joy, or worry. You don't just "get" their perspective; you share their emotional state (at least briefly).
3. **Compassionate Empathy**: Taking it further by wanting to help, offering comfort, or taking supportive action when appropriate.

Each level has its place. Cognitive Empathy can help us in negotiations or problem-solving, while emotional Empathy fosters closeness in personal relationships. Compassionate Empathy leads us to take meaningful steps to relieve another's distress.

Techniques to Boost Empathy

- **Active Listening**

This means giving someone your undivided attention. Do not text under the table or formulate your response before they finish speaking.

Offer cues that you're engaged, like nodding or reflecting on their statements. For instance, if they say, "I've been feeling overwhelmed at work," respond with, "It sounds like there's a lot on your plate right now.

Do you want to talk about what's most stressful?"

- **Perspective-Taking**

When you catch yourself judging or dismissing someone's feelings, pause. Ask: *"What if I were in their shoes?"* Try to recall a time you felt similarly. This mental exercise helps break down barriers, reminding you that emotions often have their own logic.

- **Mindful Observation**

Sometimes, people don't articulate their emotions verbally. Pay attention to body language, facial expressions, and tone of voice. Notice if someone fidgets, avoids eye contact, or speaks more softly than usual. These cues can offer insights into their emotional state.

- **Managing Self-Care**

There's a balance: empathizing with others shouldn't mean drowning in their problems. If you find Empathy draining—especially if you're a "highly sensitive person"—practice setting emotional boundaries. After a deep conversation, you might need some alone time, a short walk, or a grounding ritual like deep breathing.

Empathy in Conflict Resolution

Conflict escalates when people feel unheard or misunderstood.

Often, just showing Empathy can diffuse tension. Instead of instantly defending your position, restate the other person's concerns.

For example: "I hear that you feel overlooked when decisions are made without your input.

That sounds frustrating. Can we explore a way to keep you in the loop?"

This approach doesn't mean you agree; it just shows you value their viewpoint.

Once people feel heard, they're generally more willing to engage in solutions rather than arguments.

A Quick Exercise: The Empathy Check-In

Next time you're in a conversation—be it with a friend, family member, or colleague—ask yourself mid-way:

1. **Am I truly listening, or am I waiting to talk?**
2. **What emotions is this person experiencing right now, and why?**
3. **Is there a way I can validate their feelings, even if I don't share them?**

By pausing to reflect, you'll catch yourself when you slip into autopilot.

Over time, you'll become more adept at intuitively sensing others' emotional landscapes, fostering more profound and meaningful connections.

Having explored the power of empathy, let's move to the final subchapter: nurturing the relationships we care about most, ensuring they continue to flourish in a chaotic world.

13.3 NURTURING YOUR RELATIONSHIPS

Relationships as Living Entities

Think of your relationships as living, breathing entities that require care, attention, and adjustment over time.

Neglected relationships, like unwatered houseplants, can wither even if their foundations were once strong.

Conversely, consistent effort—no matter how small—can revive connections that seemed all but lost.

Nurturing relationships doesn't have to be time-consuming or grandiose. Simple, genuine acts can keep the emotional soil rich and fertile.

A quick text saying, "Thinking of you," a weekly coffee date, or the occasional thoughtful gift can all act as water and sunlight for the friendships and partnerships you value.

Consistency matters more than drama.

Communication: The Lifeline

You might have guessed it: communication is the cornerstone of healthy relationships. Yet, it's surprisingly easy to let small misunderstandings snowball into big grievances if we're not talking openly. Here are some building blocks:

- **Clarity**: Say what you mean—don't expect people to read your mind. If you need help, ask for it. If you're upset, express it calmly.

- **Consistency**: Make it a habit to check in, share updates about your life, and inquire about theirs.

- **Conflict Navigation**: Disagreements happen. Approach them by focusing on the issue, not the person. Use "I" statements to express feelings without casting blame: "I feel hurt when…" rather than "You always do this…"

Quality Time vs. Quantity Time

We often discuss "quality time," but what does that mean?

It's giving someone your entire presence—being mentally and emotionally there, not just physically.

Ten minutes of focused, heartfelt conversation can sometimes be more nourishing than an hour of distracted co-presence.

- **Tech Boundaries**: If you're out to dinner, consider putting phones away or turning them face-down. Even a few minutes of uninterrupted eye contact can foster intimacy.

- **Shared Rituals**: Weekly movie nights, daily walks, or a Sunday phone call with a long-distance friend can build comfort and reliability. The predictability of these rituals can anchor your relationship, reminding both parties that they're important enough to schedule.

Acts of Kindness and Appreciation

One of the most impactful ways to nurture a relationship is to express gratitude and appreciation.

Sometimes, we assume people "just know" we value them. But saying it out loud or showing it through small gestures can have a profound effect.

- **Verbal Praise**: A heartfelt "I really appreciate you" or "You mean a lot to me" can solidify bonds.

- **Thoughtful Gestures**: Surprise your partner by doing one of their usual chores, bring a coworker their favorite snack, or mail a goofy postcard to a friend for no reason.

- **Celebrating Milestones**: Celebrating a friend's small win at work or a personal breakthrough doesn't have to be a significant event. A tiny acknowledgment can light up their day and deepen your connection.

Handling Relationship Slumps

Even solid relationships go through rough patches—times when you or the other person might be stressed, distant, or simply preoccupied with different aspects of life.

Rather than panicking, see these periods as signals to invest more thought and care:

- **Initiate Dialogue**: A simple "Hey, I've noticed we haven't caught up lately. How are you doing?" can break the ice.

- **Offer Grace**: Sometimes, people pull away because they're dealing with personal issues. Show patience and Empathy. Don't assume it's about you.

- **Propose a Reset**: If tension has been brewing, suggest meeting for coffee or going for a walk to discuss things. Approach with curiosity rather than accusation.

Nurturing Yourself in Relationships

It might sound contradictory, but caring for your well-being is a huge part of nurturing relationships.

If you're stressed and depleted, you won't have much emotional bandwidth to offer others. Ensure you're setting boundaries, respecting your mental and emotional needs, and clearly communicating them to those around you.

This balance—looking after yourself while caring for others—creates healthier, more sustainable connections in the long run.

A Quick Exercise: The Relationship Radar

Periodically, take stock of your key relationships—romantic, familial, friendships, or professional:

1. **List them out** (the ones that truly matter or occupy your thoughts often).
2. **Give each a status**: healthy, strained, or needs attention.
3. **Brainstorm an action** for each: Send a thank-you note, schedule a lunch, or plan a weekend getaway to reconnect.

Following through on these small actions can have a ripple effect, transforming an "okay" relationship into a thriving one, or revitalizing a bond that's fallen into disrepair.

CONCLUSION TO CHAPTER 13

Connecting with Others is more than a heartwarming ideal—it's a critical pillar of emotional resilience and daily well-being.

When we feel genuinely supported, understood, and engaged with the people around us, stress loses much of its power over us.

In this chapter, we've seen how that support can come to life: through a carefully cultivated **Support Network**, a habit of **Practicing Empathy** and consistent efforts to **Nurture Our Relationships**.

But it's not just about receiving care. As you've gathered, these relationships flourish best when offering understanding, compassion, and practical help.

Genuine connection is reciprocal, an ongoing dance of give and take, listen and share. And that reciprocity is what makes them so enriching.

We don't connect simply because we want something from people; we connect because it's deeply encoded in our DNA to form communities—to face life's challenges together rather than in isolation.

So, how do you start putting all this into practice? You may message an old friend today, letting them know how much you've missed them.

Or you'll make a mindful effort to truly hear your coworker's concerns instead of rushing to your next task.

You could also block out a weekly time slot for a family catch-up call—where phones are off-limits and the focus is on genuine conversation.

Yes, breaking out of long-standing patterns might feel awkward, especially if you're used to independence or if some of your relationships have grown distant.

But remember, change doesn't need to be sweeping to be meaningful. A single heartfelt conversation can thaw months (or even years) of emotional distance.

A small gesture of kindness can open a door you assumed was locked. In the grand scheme of **Stress Less, Live More**, connections form a protective cushion, absorbing some of life's harsh blows and amplifying the joys we experience.

When we know someone has our back, we sleep a little easier. When we see the smile of a friend we've supported, we feel a rush of purpose.

When we empathize with someone's pain, we remind ourselves that we're not alone in our struggles.

This sense of shared humanity—of looking at a friend, colleague, or even a stranger and recognizing we're all trying our best—fuels our hearts and our resilience.

Forging authentic human bonds remains a radical, beautiful act in a world of distractions and digital noise.

And it just might be the key to unlocking a life where stress takes a back seat and living more—truly living—comes to the forefront.

CHAPTER 14
GROWING THROUGH CHALLENGE

INTRODUCTION

Think about the last time life threw you a curveball—maybe a big project got derailed by unforeseen complications, or a relationship hit a rough patch just when you thought everything was smooth sailing.

How did you respond? Did you feel overwhelmed, or did you sense some kernel of possibility hidden in that daunting situation?

Challenges, setbacks, and plain old bad days are an inevitable part of the human experience.

Still, there's a silver lining here: each bump in the road can become a stepping stone, a chance to grow rather than a reason to retreat.

This chapter, **Growing Through Challenges**, is all about harnessing the powerful potential within life's difficulties.

We'll begin with **Turning Setbacks into Stepping Stones** (Subchapter 14.1), uncovering how obstacles can spark creative solutions, deeper self-awareness, or surprising bursts of courage.

Next, in **Building Resilience Muscles** (Subchapter 14.2), we'll explore practical ways to strengthen our inner fortitude, so the next wave of adversity doesn't knock us flat.

Finally, we'll wrap up with **Keeping the Momentum** (Subchapter 14.3), ensuring that once we've learned these valuable lessons, we keep that growth rolling forward in daily life—long after the immediate crisis is over.

Strap in for a journey that blends humor, empathy, and a fair amount of real talk. Because the truth is, challenges can be messy.

They often bring out our insecurities, test our patience, or push our relationships to their limits.

Yet, in that very messiness, we discover who we are, what we're made of, and how we can transform stress into a catalyst for living more fully. Shall we dive in?

14.1 TURNING SETBACKS INTO STEPPING STONES

Embracing the "Plot Twist"

Imagine you're watching a thrilling movie. When the hero seems to have everything under control, a surprise twist plunges them into a precarious situation.

As an audience member, you grip the edge of your seat—this is the moment the hero truly gets tested, and you can't wait to see how they'll overcome the odds.

It's funny how, when it's our own life, we often despise plot twists, wishing everything was neatly planned and predictable.

But a good story thrives on tension and resolution, and so can we.

When a setback blindsides you—like a failed exam, a breakup, or a business deal gone sour—you can see it as random misfortune or the start of a "plot twist" that brings growth.

It's not about sugarcoating pain; it's about recognizing that adversity can be a launching pad.

We rarely evolve by staying in our comfort zones.

Instead, the friction and upheaval spurs new skills, insights, or directions.

Reframing Failure

"I have not failed. I've just found 10,000 ways that won't work," Thomas Edison allegedly said about his attempts to create the lightbulb.

While that might sound cliché, there's a truth: failure can be a feedback mechanism, teaching us what doesn't fit so we can inch closer to what does.

Still, that pep talk doesn't always soothe the sting of disappointment when you're in the thick of it.

How do we reframe failure without dismissing the genuine emotions that come with it? Start by acknowledging that feeling disappointed, frustrated, or even heartbroken when things go awry is okay.

Suppressing those feelings won't make them vanish; it'll just push them underground, where they can morph into stress or self-doubt.

Instead, name the emotion—"I'm so upset right now," "I feel embarrassed," or "I'm worried this proves I'm not good enough"—then remind yourself that an event is not an identity. Failing at a task doesn't make you a "failure."

It means the approach you took didn't yield the result you wanted. That's valuable data you can use to adapt and try again or pivot in a new direction.

Mining the Lessons

One practical technique is to imagine your setback as a teacher handing you a personalized syllabus.

Ask, *"What can I learn from this? What did I overlook or underestimate? Is there a skill or mindset I need to develop further?"*

You may have launched a side hustle, but it didn't attract customers.

Instead of blaming or giving up, dissect the experience: Were you marketing to the right audience? Did you need more feedback before going live? Did you simply need to be more patient?

Once you've identified lessons, consider writing them down.

"I learned that user testing is crucial before a product launch," or "I realized that I work best with a supportive accountability partner."

Documenting these insights transforms ephemeral frustration into tangible wisdom.

These "stepping stones" can guide your next move, whether refining your approach, shifting your goals, or even discovering a new passion you didn't consider.

Humor as a Coping Tool

It might sound odd to talk about humor when discussing life's setbacks. Still, laughter can be a surprisingly powerful ally in difficult times.

When the tension's thick and everything seems dark, a well-timed joke or a comedic perspective can break the mental spiral.

It's not about making light of genuine pain but rather about poking fun at our human tendency to catastrophize.

"Well," you might say to yourself, "I guess I won't be winning Employee of the Month after spilling coffee on the boss's new carpet—on the bright side, at least I gave the office a new conversation topic!"

Humor loosens the mental grip of fear and self-criticism. It reminds us that we're resilient and capable of bouncing back.

You might even share your fiasco with friends playfully—like turning your worst day into a humorous anecdote.

In that moment, you're reclaiming narrative control: yes, you faced a setback, but you can still find moments of levity and connection.

A Quick Exercise: The Setback Story

Step 1: Recall a recent setback—big or small.

Step 2: Write a brief "narrative" about it as though telling a friend what happened, how you felt, and what you did next.

Step 3: Rewrite the narrative, casting yourself as the resourceful protagonist who overcame (or is in the process of overcoming) the challenge. Add a touch of humor or a triumphant tone.

Step 4: Notice how this reframing affects your emotional state and your sense of possibility moving forward.

By practicing this exercise, you're training your brain to see setbacks as part of a dynamic story—one in which you have the agency to grow, adapt, and even lighten the mood along the way.

Having explored how to transform roadblocks into stepping stones, let's move on to the next stage: **Building Resilience Muscles** so we can handle the inevitable bumps with more grit and grace.

14.2 BUILDING RESILIENCE MUSCLES

What Does "Resilience" Really Mean?

We hear the term *resilience* tossed around often—as if it's some superpower we can magically tap into. But resilience isn't about being unbreakable.

It's about bouncing back, adapting, and even thriving after adversity.

Think of a flexible tree that sways in a storm without snapping. It doesn't resist the wind; it moves with it, relying on deep roots to keep from toppling over.

That's the essence of resilience: *adaptability + core stability*.

But guess what? Most of us aren't born with unwavering resilience.

We must build and reinforce it, like muscles that strengthen with every "workout" of adversity.

Traits of Resilient People

When we observe highly resilient individuals—be they entrepreneurs, athletes, or single parents juggling multiple jobs—we often notice common patterns:

- **Optimistic Realism**: They acknowledge challenges without giving in to despair. They see obstacles clearly but believe in their capacity to navigate them.

- **Emotional Regulation**: They don't get upset; they process emotions effectively, preventing them from spiraling into paralysis.

- **Growth Mindset**: Instead of viewing difficulties as dead ends, they see them as puzzles to solve or opportunities to learn.

- **Strong Support Networks**: They don't try to handle everything alone. They enlist help, gather mentors, or confide in friends.

You might recognize some of these traits in yourself already. Or perhaps you see areas where you could use some "strength training."

Either way, building resilience is a journey, not a destination.

Strategies for Resilience Training

- **Mental Rehearsal**

Ever watch a professional athlete close their eyes before a big event, visualizing each move? That's mental rehearsal. You can do the same for stressful situations.

If you're anticipating a difficult conversation or a nerve-wracking presentation, imagine handling it calmly. Visualize potential twists—maybe the person gets upset or asks tough questions—and see yourself responding gracefully.

This mental pre-game can lower your anxiety and help you pivot more smoothly when the actual moment arrives.

- **Healthy Boundaries**

Saying "no" sometimes (or at least "not now") isn't just about time management—it's about emotional self-care.

Overcommitting can drain our energy, leaving us with fewer resources when real crises hit. Resilient people know their limits and protect them.

They don't see it as selfishness but as preserving the mental and emotional bandwidth needed to handle life's bigger storms.

- **Physical and Emotional Self-Care**

It's hard to be resilient if you're running on fumes. Regular exercise, decent sleep, and balanced nutrition provide the biological foundation for a strong stress response.

Emotional self-care—like journaling, meditating, or engaging in hobbies—helps keep your internal world calm and centered. When adversity strikes, a well-rested, well-nourished, emotionally stable "you" stands a far better chance of weathering the storm.

- **Reframing "I Have To" Into "I Get To"**

This mindset shift might feel small but can dramatically change your outlook. Instead of lamenting, "I have to work late," try thinking, "I get to sharpen my skills or earn extra to support my family."

Instead of "I have to deal with this conflict," think, "I get to practice communication and boundary-setting."

You're flipping the narrative from victimhood to opportunity, which naturally cultivates resilience.

- **Celebrating Micro-Wins**

We often focus on the big picture, forgetting that resilience is built by acknowledging small victories.

Did you handle a tense email calmly? That's a win. Did you resist the urge to vent angrily on social media? Another win.

Each small act of self-control or problem-solving adds a brick to your resilient foundation, reinforcing the belief that you can manage adversity one step at a time.

Navigating Doubts and Setbacks in Resilience-Building

As you strengthen your resilience, you might fall back into old patterns or momentarily crumble under a new stressor.

That's normal. Building resilience doesn't mean you'll never have a meltdown or a moment of self-doubt.

It means you'll recover faster and draw lessons from each stumble.

When you notice self-criticism creeping in—*"I thought I was more resilient than this!"*—remind yourself that progress isn't linear.

That's okay. Each experience can be added to your "resilience training log," fueling your long-term growth.

A Quick Exercise: The Resilience Ledger

Step 1: Take a sheet of paper and create two columns: "Challenges Faced" and "How I Overcame."

Step 2: List past difficulties—big or small—and write how you resolved or endured them.

Step 3: Notice patterns: Did you rely on certain coping strategies, people, or inner qualities?

Step 4: Keep the ledger handy. Next time a new obstacle appears, glance at how you've handled past hurdles. This reminds you: "I've bounced back before and can do it again."

By actively building your resilience muscles, you won't just survive life's storms—you'll harness them as catalysts for growth. But once you've tasted some success—once you've begun turning setbacks into learning opportunities and developed a more resilient stance—how do you maintain that momentum? Next: **Keeping the Momentum.**

14.3 KEEPING THE MOMENTUM

Why We Lose Steam

Ever start a new habit or mindset shift with gusto, only to find your enthusiasm waning after a few weeks? You're not alone.

Life is busy, distractions abound, and it's easy for the changes we make—no matter how valuable—to slip onto the back burner.

However, sustaining growth is crucial, mainly when you aim to handle stress more effectively and live more efficiently.

Suppose we let our newfound resilience or positive outlook fade away. In that case, we risk sliding back into old patterns when the next challenge hits.

The Value of Mini Check-Ins

One of the best ways to keep momentum is by weaving *regular check-ins* into your routine. Think of these as pit stops in a marathon. You're not stopping the race; you're just refueling.

You can do this weekly, bi-weekly, or monthly—whatever fits your life.

During a mini check-in, ask yourself:

1. **What did I learn about myself this past week (or month)?**
2. **Where did I handle stress well, and where did I stumble?**
3. **What new or ongoing challenges am I facing, and how can I apply my resilience toolkit?**

Write down your thoughts or discuss them with a friend. You might discover you're doing better than you realized or pinpoint areas where you need to tweak your strategy.

Consistent self-awareness fosters a sense of direction and accountability, making you less likely to drift.

Setting Evolving Goals

Have you ever aimed for a specific goal—like improving communication in your relationship or meditating daily—and then, after reaching it, wondered, *"Now what?"*

That's a classic momentum killer: hitting a milestone but failing to set the next one. Instead, treat each accomplishment as a stepping stone toward something more significant.

If you've successfully meditated for five minutes a day for a month, maybe now you can extend it to ten minutes or add a mindful walking session.

If your communication with your spouse has improved, consider tackling the next challenge—like scheduling a weekly date night to keep the bond strong.

Goals don't have to be monumental. Sometimes, the best momentum-building targets are modest increments—slightly deeper, more refined versions of what you're already doing well.

The key is to stay curious about where you can go next.

Rewarding Progress

Humans are wired to respond to rewards. It's how our brain's dopamine system keeps us motivated.

So, don't wait for a grand finale to celebrate. Did you manage to calmly navigate a tense situation at work? Did you keep up your journaling habit for two weeks straight?

Reward yourself—even if it's just with a symbolic gesture like treating yourself to a special tea or taking an hour for a hobby you love.

These micro-rewards serve as "thank you" notes to your brain, reinforcing the habits you want to stick to.

Harnessing Social Accountability

Remember that growth thrives in the community. If you struggle to maintain momentum on your own, invite a friend, coworker, or family member to join you in your quest for resilience and stress reduction.

Share updates or set joint goals. Maybe every Monday morning, you send each other a quick text: "What's your focus for resilience this week?" or "How did you handle the weekend's challenges?"

This mutual check-in can keep you both on track and inject a sense of camaraderie into your journey.

Don't forget online communities or support groups if in-person buddies are scarce.

Sometimes, posting a brief update in a Facebook group or forum can keep you accountable and inspire others who read about your progress.

Integrating Growth into Identity

One of the most powerful ways to maintain momentum is to incorporate your new habits or perspectives into your identity.

Instead of saying, "I'm trying to be more resilient," say, "I am a resilient person who keeps learning."

Instead of, "I'm attempting to manage stress better," say, "I'm the kind of person who invests in my emotional well-being."

That subtle shift in language can make a huge difference in how you approach everyday decisions.

When resilience and stress management become part of who you are, you're more likely to stand by them, just as you wouldn't abandon core aspects of your personality.

Handling Setbacks as Part of the Process

No matter how well you plan, life will occasionally knock you off course. A personal crisis may arise, or you simply have unproductive days.

The secret is to view these lapses not as "failures" but as part of the ongoing process.

A missed meditation session or a meltdown at work doesn't erase weeks of progress; it's just a signal to revisit what's working and what needs adjusting.

Next time you slip up, tell yourself, "Okay, that happened. How do I get back on track with the knowledge I've gained?"

A Quick Exercise: Future-Focused Visualization

1. **Close your eyes** (or keep them softly open if that's more comfortable). Imagine six months from now—you've been consistently applying the lessons from this book and your personal growth efforts.
2. **Visualize:** Imagine yourself handling challenges calmly, noticing your stress levels drop more quickly, and feeling confident in your ability to bounce back.
3. **Feel:** Soak up how that future version of you feels. Is there lightness in your chest? A sense of accomplishment? Relief?

4. **Open your eyes:** Jot down a few words that sum up that sensation. Use those words as a mini-mantra to remind yourself why you maintain these habits and mindsets.

This small visualization keeps you connected to the "why" behind your journey, fueling your motivation to keep building on what you've started.

CONCLUSION TO CHAPTER 14

When life challenges our way, hiding under the covers or moping about how unfair the world can be is tempting.

But as we've explored in **"Growing Through Challenges,"** adversity doesn't have to be a roadblock; it can be the very path that leads us to new depths of strength, compassion, and creativity.

In **Turning Setbacks into Stepping Stones**, we saw how to reclaim our narrative during tough times—shifting from "Why me?" to "What can I learn here?"

We discovered the power of reframing failure as feedback, letting humor dissolve tension, and writing our personal "setback story" in a way that spotlights our resilience rather than our defeat.

Then we dived into **Building Resilience Muscles**.

We recognized that resilience isn't about never feeling shaken—it's about how quickly we regain our footing.

By cultivating traits like optimistic realism, emotional regulation, and a growth mindset—and by practicing strategies like mental rehearsal, boundary-setting, and self-care—we become better equipped to handle future storms.

Each trial becomes a "workout" that strengthens our capacity to face whatever life might throw next.

Finally, in **Keeping the Momentum**, we addressed the all-important question: *Once we start growing, how do we not lose steam?*

We learned to schedule mini-check-ins, set evolving goals, reward small wins, and draw on social accountability to keep ourselves moving forward.

Integrating our newfound resilience into our identity transforms fleeting breakthroughs into long-lasting change.

At this point, you might be wondering, *"So, what now?"*

The simplest answer is: keep going. Implement just one idea from this chapter—maybe the "Setback Story" exercise or the "Resilience Ledger"—and see where it takes you.

Or schedule a weekly check-in with a friend to share micro-wins. Even a small step can start a ripple of positive changes that build upon each other.

Let's also acknowledge the complexity of real life. Challenges can be layered—financial pressures, family obligations, personal losses—and not every hurdle comes with a neat lesson.

Some difficulties are brutal, and needing professional help or leaning heavily on your support network is okay.

Recognizing that doesn't invalidate our capacity to grow; it brings nuance.

Sometimes resilience means bravely seeking outside resources.

Sometimes, it means taking a break to gather your strength before pushing forward again.

Yet, across the board, the overarching message stands: tough times can be catalysts.

You have the choice, at every turn, to see a setback as a crushing weight or as a stepping stone—even if it's a rough, jagged one.

You can cultivate resilience, reframe obstacles, and maintain forward momentum in ways that might surprise you.

Doing so brings you closer to a life where stress doesn't call all the shots, and "living more" becomes your new normal.

So the next time you face a challenge—minor or monumental—try smiling at the "plot twist."

Let the world do its worst, and then show it your best.

Because you're not just surviving; you're growing.

And there's no limit to how strong, wise, and vibrant you can become when you refuse to let setbacks define you.

CHAPTER 15
LIVING IN FULLNESS

INTRODUCTION

Picture yourself standing at the edge of a vast, peaceful ocean at dawn. The sky unfolds in brilliant pinks and oranges, reflecting over calm water.

You take a deep breath, inhaling the crisp air, and feel a subtle sense of awe stirring in your chest. At that moment, you're not worried about your inbox, bank account, or meeting scheduled next week.

You're just there—fully present, alive, and part of something bigger than your daily stresses.

That is a glimpse of **living in Fullness**.

But what does "living in fullness" really mean? We could define it as recognizing the richness and possibility in each day, even when life is imperfect or messy.

It's not about amassing material luxuries or achieving grand feats that prompt applause from the crowd—though those can be nice.

Instead, it's about nurturing a relationship with yourself, your life, and the people around you that celebrates the beauty and wonder already present.

This final chapter, **"Living in Fullness,"** intends to weave together all the insights, tools, and reflections you've encountered.

We'll start by exploring **Honoring Your Journey** (Subchapter 15.1), acknowledging how every step—yes, even the stumbles—leads you toward a life less driven by stress and more guided by self-awareness.

Then, in **Sustaining Peace and Love** (Subchapter 15.2), we'll look at how to keep your sense of calm and compassion alive over the long haul rather than letting it fizzle when challenges return.

Finally, we'll consider **Ongoing Evolution** (Subchapter 15.3), recognizing that this journey is never "complete" in a conventional sense. We're all works in progress, continually unfolding, moment by moment.

So, let's begin by stepping onto that metaphorical shoreline of your life, where the ocean of possibilities greets you with each sunrise.

You've come a long way and have even more room to grow, breathe, laugh, and savor. Ready? Let's dive in.

15.1 HONORING YOUR JOURNEY

The Power of Reflection

Imagine leafing through a scrapbook of your life, filled with photographs of the highlight moments—graduations, vacations, birthday parties—and the less glamorous days.

The days you were frustrated, confused, or feeling a tad lost.

This scrapbook might also include the small wins nobody else knew about: the time you spoke kindly to yourself instead of being critical or the first morning you managed to do a five-minute meditation without your mind wandering off too much.

These pages, from the messy to the triumphant, form your unique path.

Honoring your journey means looking back on all those pages with a sense of respect and gratitude rather than regret or shame. Sure, there might be cringe-worthy episodes.

Perhaps you remember times when you lashed out at someone you love or believed you were unworthy of something wonderful.

But each of these moments has shaped you, taught you lessons, and nudged you forward.

Why Reflection Helps You Stress Less

Reflection isn't about dwelling on the past with remorse. It's about acknowledging your development.

When you see how far you've come—how your mindset, habits, or relationships have evolved—you cultivate a sense of possibility. Maybe you made mistakes, but you also made changes. Perhaps you doubted yourself, yet you persisted anyway.

This retrospective awareness can fortify you against current and future stressors by reminding you that you've adapted and can do it again.

Journaling Your Evolution

If you've ever kept a journal, you might notice how your writing from months or years ago seems to belong to a different person. You see the old worries and the previous coping mechanisms and realize how much has shifted.

If you haven't kept a journal, you can still start now—or write a short retrospective piece:

- **List** five ways you've changed in the past few years—emotionally, mentally, spiritually, or physically.
- **Acknowledge** which challenges spurred those changes.
- **Note** any surprise benefits or byproducts you gained from the process.

This practice can be deeply affirming. It also shows that you're capable of continuous growth—even when you felt stuck or hopeless, you moved forward.

Embracing All the Versions of You

One thing about honoring your journey is recognizing that you've worn many hats or inhabited various identities: the worried student, the newlywed bursting with optimism, the overwhelmed parent, the job-seeker, the friend in a crisis, or maybe all of the above in different chapters of your life.

Each of those past "yous" deserves compassion and acceptance. Each played a role in shaping who you are now.

This acceptance helps you let go of the stress of trying to hide or erase old versions of yourself. Instead, you hold them gently, whispering, "Thank you for getting me here. I've learned so much."

A Gentle Exercise: The Life Timeline

1. **Draw a horizontal line** across a sheet of paper, marking your birth on the left and the present moment on the right.
2. **Plot key events** along this timeline—the significant milestones (graduations, jobs, relationships) and smaller turning points (like discovering a stress-management technique that helped or deciding to speak up for yourself in a challenging situation).
3. **Reflect** on each event: What did it teach you about yourself, others, and life? How did it shape your perspective on stress and fulfillment?

You might notice that even "negative" experiences gave you something—maybe resilience, empathy, or a newfound sense of priorities.

The Ongoing Nature of Self-Discovery

We don't reach a magical end where we say, "Welp, I've honored my journey enough. Time to check out."

Each new day brings possibilities for further understanding.

The difference is that you stop racing anxiously toward a finish line once you begin practicing mindful reflection and self-compassion.

You become more present in the unfolding of your life, with all its twists and turns. And that presence is precisely what can ease stress.

When you're not busy condemning your past or obsessing over a future "perfect self," you free up mental space to handle what's in front of you now—with clarity and joy.

From this vantage, you're better prepared to maintain the peace and love you've been cultivating. Let's explore that in Subchapter 15.2.

15.2 SUSTAINING PEACE AND LOVE

Why Peace Feels Elusive Sometimes

Have you ever woken up after a great day, feeling calm and full of appreciation, only to find that a minor argument or a frustrating email has shattered your sense of peace by lunchtime?

The fleeting nature of peace can be disheartening. We might think it appears randomly, like a hummingbird that flits into our backyard for a moment before darting away.

However, **sustaining peace and love** isn't about clutching them so tightly that they never change—it's about creating conditions that make them more likely to thrive.

Like tending a garden, you can't force a plant to grow but can provide fertile soil, water, and sunlight.

Building a Peaceful Routine

One of the most straightforward paths to sustained peace is to weave calming practices into your daily life—habits that keep your stress levels from boiling over. Here are a few:

- **Morning Stillness**: Even if it's just three minutes, sit quietly with your coffee or tea, focusing on your breath rather than your phone. This gentle act can anchor your day in calmness.

- **Mindful Transitions**: When you move from one activity to another—like finishing work and starting personal time—take a moment to reset. Exhale the tension, literally or metaphorically. This slight pause helps you avoid carrying stress from one realm of life into another.

- **Scheduled Breaks**: Make a reminder on your calendar or phone to stand up and stretch. Do a quick breathing exercise or a short gratitude reflection. These micro-breaks maintain an undercurrent of peace all day.

At first, these might feel too trivial to matter. But over time, they accumulate, forming a protective net that catches you before stress escalates.

The Role of Love (Toward Self and Others)

When we say "love," it's easy to think of grand romantic gestures or familial devotion.

But in a broader sense, love is an active stance of kindness, patience, and empathy—applied to yourself as much as to anyone else.

Maintaining love means consistently checking in with the question: *"Am I responding to myself and others with compassion, or am I letting fear, irritation, or judgment lead the way?"*

- **Self-Love**: Not the narcissistic "I'm better than everyone" kind, but the gentle assurance that you are worthy of care, rest, and forgiveness. This helps you stress less because you're less prone to beating yourself up.
- **Interpersonal Love**: Extending warmth to friends, family, or strangers fosters positive connections. And positive connections reinforce your sense of safety and support—a vital buffer against stress.

Bouncing Back from Conflict

You might wonder: "What about when my sense of love and peace gets disrupted by real-world conflicts, arguments, or betrayals?"

That's inevitable. The key is how quickly you can return to a place of equanimity.

- **Pause and Breathe**: When tension flares, give yourself a beat to slow your racing mind.
- **Name the Feeling**: "I'm feeling angry," "I'm feeling hurt," etc. This self-awareness calms your nervous system.
- **Seek Understanding**: Before jumping to conclusions, try seeing the situation from the other person's perspective. This doesn't justify harmful behavior but can soften the edges of conflict.
- **Repair the Connection**: If a conversation goes poorly, find the time (when emotions have settled) to approach the person and express your desire to reconnect or resolve the issue peacefully.

Peace and love aren't about never experiencing tension or negative emotions. They're about having reliable ways to return to balance when life tips you off-kilter.

Cultivating Love in Simple Acts

Extensive declarations of affection have their place, but small, regular demonstrations of care often speak louder.

That might look like:

- **Sending a thoughtful text** to a friend who's having a rough week.
- **Sharing a meal** with someone you appreciate, with no agenda other than enjoying each other's company.
- **Complimenting yourself** out loud when you do something kind or brave reinforces self-love in real-time.

Day by day, these gentle gestures keep your emotional ecosystem healthy and help you navigate stress with a fuller heart.

And as you nurture this sense of peace and love, you'll notice yourself evolving—becoming calmer and more open and curious.

That's where the next subchapter—**Ongoing Evolution**—comes into play.

15.3 ONGOING EVOLUTION

The Myth of a "Finished" Self

Sometimes, we operate as though there's a finish line for personal growth—some magical moment when we become fully actualized, never to struggle again.

In reality, growth is constantly unfolding. You can always discover new facets of your personality, adopt new skills, or refine the qualities you admire in yourself.

At each life stage, new challenges and roles might emerge—becoming a parent, switching careers, relocating to a new city—and fresh opportunities to adapt and learn.

Rather than feeling that you must "arrive" at perfection, consider yourself a **work in progress**—beautiful, flawed, and always capable of transformation.

Accepting you'll never be "done" can ease stress because you free yourself from the burden of chasing a static ideal.

Instead, you remain open to growth as life naturally unfolds.

Continuous Learning

Ongoing evolution thrives on curiosity. *"What more can I learn about this topic, skill, or part of myself?"* Curiosity infuses your daily experiences with excitement, turning mundane routines into mini-labs for experimentation.

Maybe you decide to learn a new language or practice a new hobby—both can rejuvenate your mind and give you a sense of forward motion.

In a world brimming with digital resources, you can find tutorials, online communities, and mentors for almost anything—cooking, coding, painting, you name it.

By consistently engaging in small learning goals, you keep your brain flexible and adaptable, shielding you from the stagnation and stress that come from feeling stuck.

Embracing the Seasonality of Life

We often talk about life as a series of chapters or seasons. You might be in a season of intense focus on your career, followed by a season of family responsibilities, and later, a season of personal exploration or retirement.

Each season invites different expressions of who you are. Understanding this cyclical nature can prevent you from clinging too tightly to any one role or identity.

For instance, if you're in a demanding work season, you might stress less by acknowledging this is temporary—you're learning a lot and earning what you need.

Eventually, you'll shift into a different gear.

If you're in a quieter season (maybe you've scaled back on commitments), that might be your chance to deepen self-care or relationships.

Letting seasons flow can remove the guilt or frustration of not "doing it all" at once.

Adapting to New Stressors

Your evolution means new challenges will arise.

Maybe you develop resilience to specific triggers (like public speaking) but discover other stressors (like caring for aging parents) you haven't faced before. This is normal.

Each new stressor is a chance to use or refine the tools you've been gathering—mindful breathing, boundary-setting, communication skills, etc.

Over time, you amass a versatile "toolkit" for a broader range of life's complexities.

Self-Compassion in the Face of Imperfection

When you're constantly evolving, you're bound to trip up.

Perhaps you've told yourself to keep a daily gratitude practice, only to forget it for two weeks straight. Or maybe you vow to handle conflicts calmly but lose your temper during a tense conversation.

These slip-ups are part of growth. Instead of labeling them as "failure," see them as data points: they reveal areas needing revisiting or strategies needing tweaking.

Ask: *"What got in the way? Was I overwhelmed, distracted, or lacking support? How can I adjust next time?"* This gentle approach helps you improve and keeps your stress levels in check—because you're not piling guilt on top of an already challenging situation.

Balancing Acceptance and Aspiration

Ongoing evolution doesn't mean you can't accept and love yourself as you are right now. There's a powerful balance between **contentment** and **aspiration**: appreciating your current self while recognizing you still have room to grow.

That healthy tension fuels a sense of excitement for what lies ahead without demeaning your present worth.

- **Acceptance**: "I'm okay where I am—my feelings and experiences are valid."
- **Aspiration**: "I also have the potential to expand my understanding, refine my behavior, and achieve new levels of peace or skill."

When you hold both truths, you maintain a healthy perspective.

Stress decreases because you don't beat yourself up for every perceived shortfall or ignore the possibilities for improvement.

A Quick Exercise: The Growth Spiral

1. **Draw a spiral** on paper, starting at the center and circling outward.
2. **Label each coil** with an aspect of your life—relationships, career, personal habits, emotional health, etc.
3. **Write** how you've evolved in that area next to each coil and how you would like to evolve further.
4. **Note** that the spiral keeps expanding, indicating you'll keep looping back with new insights each time.

This visual helps you see your life as a continuous unfolding.

This spiral widens and deepens rather than a one-way line that abruptly ends.

CONCLUSION TO CHAPTER 15

Living in Fullness isn't a final destination you reach with a grand flourish; it's an ongoing way of engaging with life.

Honoring Your Journey taught you the importance of embracing every chapter—victories, blunders, and all—as part of the entity that makes you who you are.

Doing so will lighten the load of regret or self-judgment and create a foundation of self-respect that staves off needless stress.

In **Sustaining Peace and Love**, we explored practical ways to maintain a calm, compassionate mindset in daily life.

Through small, consistent actions—like morning stillness, mindful transitions, and conscious acts of kindness—you cultivate a steady undercurrent of warmth for yourself and others.

That sense of love and tranquility becomes a refuge you can return to when turbulence arises.

Finally, **Ongoing Evolution** reminded us that growth is perpetual, shaped by curiosity, adaptability, and a willingness to meet life's new chapters with a blend of acceptance and aspiration.

You're not "done" at any particular milestone; you keep learning, unlearning, refining, and unfolding.

Stress lessening becomes a dynamic process, not a single achievement. It's the consistent choice to adapt, reflect, and expand your coping strategies as life evolves.

Bringing It All Together

If you were to stitch together a single quilt from this entire book, each chapter would represent a different square, each colored by its theme—mindfulness, boundaries, self-compassion, resilience, and so on.

Living in Fullness is the binding that holds all these patches together, forming a coherent, vibrant whole. Every practice—whether it's journaling your small wins, taking mindful mini-breaks, or setting healthy boundaries—contributes a distinct thread.

An Invitation for the Road Ahead

As you close this chapter (and perhaps this book), I invite you to take one final, gentle breath.

Allow your shoulders to relax and your mind to settle. Reflect on everything you've gleaned: the insights, the aha moments, the simple tips you plan to implement.

Then, ask yourself:

- **What is one tangible step** I can take today—right now—to embody a life of Fullness?
- **Which practice or perspective** resonates so strongly that I want to make it part of my routine?
- **How can I remind myself** I have tools and a support network to guide me back to the center even when stress flares?

No matter what you choose—perhaps writing a quick gratitude note, texting a loved one, or simply sipping your next cup of tea mindfully—let it be an act of commitment to this path.

The everyday, seemingly small gestures knit together into a grand experience of well-being and joy.

Because here's a secret: **Living in Fullness** isn't reserved for the ultra-enlightened or the impeccably disciplined.

It's for anyone willing to pause, notice beauty, cultivate peace, and keep evolving.

It's for those who stumble but get back up, laugh at themselves when they realize they're taking life too seriously, and don't shy away from their vulnerabilities because they understand those tender spots are where the light can truly shine through.

And that, dear reader, is how you **stress less** and **live more**: by honoring your messy, beautiful journey, by tending to peace and love like cherished plants in your garden, and by welcoming ongoing evolution as the natural, thrilling ride it is.

May you continue to unfold, radiate kindness toward yourself and others, and greet each new day with the sense that *Fullness* is not just a goal but a practice—a way of being—within your constant reach.

AFTERWORD

Allow yourself a gentle pause right now, wherever you are. Take a slow breath. Close your eyes if that feels comfortable.

Do you sense any shift in your body—a slight drop in tension in your shoulders, a release in your jaw, or a calmer, less frantic hum of thoughts?

If you've followed along with this book's chapters, you've likely become more attuned to your patterns and responses, more conscious of how you carry stress, and more knowledgeable about practical steps to lighten your load.

Think of this moment as a door closing on an old chapter and opening onto a new horizon—one where you stress less and truly **live more**.

Hello, dear reader, and welcome to the **Afterword** of *Stress Less, Live More–A Mindful Path to Instant Anxiety Relief and Emotional Resilience*.

It's where we wrap up our collective explorations, reflect on the journey you and I have taken together, and lay out a bright canvas of possibility for what comes next.

You've braved many topics, from discovering inner calm, building boundaries, and practicing self-compassion to turning adversity into growth and finding moments of delight in the smallest corners of daily life.

We stand together at this concluding threshold, ready to fold these lessons into your everyday reality.

Imagine you're leaving a cozy workshop you've attended for a while—your notebook is brimming with scribbled insights and personal reflections, your mind whirls with fresh perspectives, and your heart hums with a sense of optimism.

You exit the workshop door, step onto the sunlit street, and realize: *"This is where the real test begins. How do I apply all these ideas?"*

The Afterword aims to serve as that final handshake with your instructor, that warm wave goodbye that reminds you of the tools in your possession and spurs you to keep practicing—because transformation blooms through action, repetition, and curiosity.

Looking Back to Look Ahead

One of the biggest pitfalls in personal development is racing through knowledge and then shelving it away, never fully practicing what you've learned.

Think about the times you bought a self-help book, read it cover to cover, felt the adrenaline rush of "Yes, this will change my life," and then... returned to your usual routine by Monday.

No judgment here—this pattern is typical, especially when daily life is jam-packed with obligations.

But suppose you want to see tangible shifts in how you respond to stress, navigate relationships, or sustain compassion and peace.

In that case, you need to transform these chapters from mere reading into living.

Pause for a moment and reflect: which chapters resonated with you most strongly?

Were you especially drawn to the concepts of mindfulness and mini-breaks?

Did the idea of journaling or daily gratitude light a spark in your heart?

Maybe boundary-setting and self-compassion were the skills you realized you've been craving all along.

Or perhaps you found resonance in the latter sections about resilience and continuous growth.

Whichever sections stirred your emotions or gave you an "aha" moment, hold on to them.

Mark those pages, revisit the strategies, and consider weaving them into your next week's routine.

This backward glance is not to dwell on the past but to glean the gems that could pave the way for your immediate future.

The best way to cultivate any newly discovered tool is to re-encounter it frequently, let it marinate in your consciousness, and then apply it in real scenarios—like conflict resolution, decision-making, or self-care.

That's how you bridge the gap between concept and reality and transform ephemeral reading pleasure into genuine life change.

Embracing Imperfection and Uncertainty

Let's be honest: even with the best intentions, you'll have days when stress rears its head forcefully or old habits resurface at the worst moments.

You might find yourself snapping at a loved one despite your newfound empathy training or ignoring your own boundaries even though you vowed to uphold them.

This can feel discouraging as if you're failing or undermining all the progress you've made.

But here's the thing: real growth doesn't follow a straight, upward path.

It's more of a spiral with dips and rises, a messy swirl of improvements and relapses.

When you catch yourself regressing or fumbling, remember to breathe.

Invite that gentle self-compassion you've been practicing: *"I notice I'm reverting to my old stress reaction. That's okay. I can pause and reset."*

This tender approach to mistakes is not about making excuses; it's about acknowledging that you're human, living in a complex world that doesn't always dance to the tune of your well-intentioned plans.

Each so-called setback can serve as a nudge to realign, to try again with a bit more awareness.

Uncertainty is also part of the equation. In a sense, you can never be entirely sure how you'll respond to a future crisis or what curveballs life will hurl at you.

But the teachings in this book equip you with a toolkit that expands your possibilities.

Instead of defaulting to panic, you have breathing techniques, journaling exercises, mindful communication strategies, and more.

So when uncertainty looms, remember: you don't have to be perfect; just be prepared enough to give yourself a fighting chance at staying calm and open.

Making the Exercises Your Own

Throughout this book, you've encountered various exercises—like body scans, gratitude journaling, empathy-building dialogues, boundary-setting scripts, or mini-break adventures.

By now, you might have dabbled in some or most of them or just read about them and thought, "Huh, that's neat."

To truly benefit, consider adopting at least one or two exercises as part of your routine.

How might you do that? Let's brainstorm:

- **Habit-Stacking**: Tuck a new practice onto an existing habit. For example, if you already brush your teeth each morning, you could add a quick two-minute visualization of your day's highlights while you rinse your mouth.
- **Scheduling**: Pick a consistent time for mindfulness or journaling—right before bed or first thing in the morning.
- **Group Accountability**: Share your chosen exercise with a friend or partner, and set up a brief check-in, like "Hey, did you do your five-minute gratitude write-up today?"
- **Tech Reminders**: Use a digital calendar or app for gentle prompts. For example, set a daily alarm at 9 p.m. that says, "Mini reflection time—note three joys from today."

The idea is not to overload yourself but to integrate these techniques seamlessly so they become second nature.

Over time, the initial effort of remembering or forcing yourself to do them will fade, replaced by a comforting routine you'll even look forward to.

The Strength of Supportive Communities

One often undervalued resource in personal growth is community—people who "get it," who can share the highs and lows of trying to stress less and live more.

If you haven't already, consider finding or forming a supportive group, in-person or online, to exchange tips, successes, and even comedic fails.

- **Join or Start a "Mindful Living Circle"**: This is a small circle of friends who gather weekly or monthly to discuss experiences, share new strategies, and hold each other accountable.
- **Leverage Online Platforms**: Many forums or social media groups focus on mindfulness, stress management, and self-compassion. Engaging there might spark new ideas and keep you motivated.
- **Buddy System**: If group settings aren't your thing, find a single buddy with similar goals. A five-minute phone check-in can do wonders for staying on track and feeling seen.

Connecting with others on the same path makes you realize you're not alone in your challenges.

The sense of camaraderie can reduce shame around slip-ups and multiply the joy of each breakthrough.

You learn from each other's successes and missteps, expanding your coping tools.

Reflecting on Relationship Growth

Since diving into these practices, have you noticed any shifts in your interactions with friends, family, or coworkers?

Perhaps you've become more attuned to empathy or catch yourself listening more patiently instead of jumping in with unsolicited advice.

You might be setting more explicit boundaries or finding more compassion in heated arguments.

Watch for these relational changes because they often provide the sweetest rewards.

It's important to celebrate these small, interpersonal wins. Maybe you managed to remain calm during a disagreement that would've historically left you seething.

Or you dared to articulate your needs without guilt.

That's huge! Over time, these incremental improvements in your relationship dynamics can drastically lower the background stress of daily life, freeing up emotional energy for more joy and creativity.

Bringing Humor and Lightness Along

If there's one aspect I hope has come through in this book, it's that personal growth doesn't have to be somber.

Stress can be deadly serious at times, but your approach to tackling it can be playful, witty, and laced with laughter.

Humor disarms tension. It's the oil that keeps the machine of growth from grinding under the weight of self-imposed pressure.

In moments of gloom or exasperation, ask yourself, *"What's one small thing I can find mildly amusing about this situation?"*

Or recall a funny memory from your past. If you're in a suitable environment (i.e., not in the middle of a stuffy board meeting), let out a tiny snort of laughter.

This isn't about ignoring the seriousness of problems but about allowing yourself to lighten the emotional load just enough to think more clearly and react more calmly.

Future Pathways: More Relationship Talents to Develop

Up to this point, we've touched on multiple ways to cultivate healthier and more supportive relationships—with yourself and others.

But the road to mastery in any relational skill is long and winding. You could delve deeper into:

- **Nonviolent Communication**: Sharpening how you express needs and feelings in conflict situations.
- **Somatic Awareness**: Learning how your body reacts in interpersonal dynamics, thereby catching tension early before it escalates.
- **Collaborative Goal-Setting**: If you live with a partner or family, co-creating shared routines or "peace rituals" can unify your approach to stress management.

- **Advanced Empathy Training**: Some programs or therapists focus specifically on developing high-level empathic listening or validation skills.

Think of each area as another door you could open, each offering a new dimension to your growth.

You might not explore them all at once, but having them on your radar broadens your horizon of possibilities.

Checking In with Your "Why"

One simple yet powerful question to revisit is: *"Why do I want to stress less and live more?"*

Maybe it's to model healthy habits for your children or to ensure your golden years are rich in experiences rather than regrets.

Perhaps you're tired of feeling burnt out and yearn for creativity to re-enter your life.

Or you simply want to savor each day more, building a mosaic of peaceful, love-filled moments.

Revisiting your "why" strengthens your motivation, especially when obstacles appear.

It helps you see the bigger picture—this isn't just about trying not to freak out at your next presentation.

It's about becoming the kind of person who greets life with curiosity, kindness, and a quiet confidence that no matter what happens, you have the resilience to face it.

Practicing Gratitude for This Journey

Please take a moment to appreciate yourself for investing in this reading journey.

Many books are started and never finished; many self-improvement ideas sparkle for a moment and fade.

But here you are, at the end of the book, reading the Afterword, which means you've shown remarkable commitment.

That's worth celebrating.

- **Thank your mind** for being open to new concepts, even if some felt a bit out of your comfort zone.
- **Thank your heart** for absorbing these lessons allowing yourself to feel inspired or vulnerable.
- **Thank your time**—yes, time is a resource—for giving space to this exploration.

When you cultivate gratitude for even the small steps you've taken, you reinforce a sense of self-worth, making it easier to keep going.

Recognizing the Ripple Effect

One beautiful byproduct of working on your own stress levels and emotional resilience is how it ripples out to others.

Think about how you might have brightened a coworker's day by staying calm in a chaotic moment or gently checking in with them during their stressed-out lunch break.

Or consider the relief your family might feel if you're not coming home frazzled daily.

When you become a calmer, more mindful presence, you inadvertently inspire the people around you to consider the possibility of a lighter existence.

This influence doesn't have to be overt. You don't need to stand on a soapbox or preach from a motivational podium.

Living your life differently—breathing through tension, pausing before reacting, genuinely listening—can set an example.

Over time, that example might encourage others to ask, "How do you stay so balanced? Can you share some tips?"

And just like that, you become a catalyst for someone else's growth.

Embracing the Complexity of Human Emotions

We also shouldn't sugarcoat life: times of pain, grief, and confusion will still come. That's part of the deal.

The difference is that now you have a more robust set of strategies for handling them with grace.

You can approach sadness or anger with curiosity, letting it be felt and expressed without letting it define your identity.

You can approach fear with caution and courage, recognizing that fear often signals an opportunity to learn or protect something precious.

So when you inevitably face heavy emotions, remember this entire book's message: stress and emotional turmoil don't have to break you.

They can be navigated, understood, and even transformed into stepping stones.

And if you falter temporarily, that's not a permanent reflection of who you are—just a moment in your ongoing dance with life's unpredictability.

Inviting You to Stay in Dialogue

An Afterword often marks the end of a reading experience.

Still, it can also start an ongoing dialogue—between you and these ideas, your environment, your friends, or a broader community.

If any question keeps pinging in your mind—"How do I adapt the journaling exercise to my chaotic schedule?" "Is there a short breathing technique for quick stress relief in traffic?"—don't let that question float away.

Seek answers. Research. Experiment. Share your successes and struggles with trusted peers.

And maybe, one day, you'll decide to revisit the book. Because personal growth is cyclical.

You might find that specific chapters resonate differently three months or a year from now because you've walked a bit further down your path.

That's the wonder of the written word: it's ready to meet you anew. However, your life circumstances have changed.

Celebrating This Moment

It's common in self-improvement literature to push for the next milestone or big leap. Let's pause on that for a second.

Right now, in this very moment, you've reached a milestone: **completing an entire book on mindful living, resilience, and stress relief.** That's no small feat.

Many individuals pick up a book, skim a few chapters, and then let it gather dust. You, however, saw it through to the end.

This decision to persevere suggests you're invested in reshaping your life to minimize unnecessary stress and maximize meaningful engagement.

Give yourself a metaphorical round of applause or a warm smile in the mirror.

Acknowledge how far you've come, not just in reading these pages but in the personal insights you've likely gained along the way.

Even if you only implemented a fraction of the techniques, you've taken active steps toward a healthier, more fulfilling existence.

That deserves recognition.

A Future Full of Open Doors

So, where do we part ways? In truth, we don't. The essence of **Stress Less, Live More** will continue to resonate within you as you head back into your routines, face challenges, or embark on new adventures.

Every moment offers a fresh chance to breathe consciously, show compassion, choose humor over frustration, or craft a gentle boundary for your sanity.

Picture your life unfolding like a series of doors. Each day, you approach a new threshold.

Sometimes, the door leads to a joyous experience, a lesson learned through adversity.

But with the knowledge and skills gleaned from this book, you're less likely to shy away or bar the door shut out of fear.

Instead, you can enter each new space with an open heart, mindful presence, and a growing self-assurance that you can handle what's inside.

Imagine the possibilities: you might discover a passion for teaching mindfulness to kids or find that your relationships blossom as you incorporate more profound empathy and listening.

The specifics are up to you.

This book never claimed to have all the answers, but it offered you tools.

Your art form is how you wield them and to what grand or humble ends.

Final Words of Encouragement

Let's round this out in a style befitting an Afterword: with heartfelt thanks and a gentle nudge.

Thank you for entrusting me (and these pages) with a slice of your time and emotional energy.

Thank you for being courageous enough to look at your stress patterns, daily habits, and vulnerabilities.

That takes guts.

And here's the nudge: *Don't let this be the final chapter of your transformation.* Keep the lessons alive in your everyday existence.

Follow your curiosity, remain open to new techniques, and continue shaping a life that reflects your values, dreams, and capacity for love.

Yes, you will get stressed. Sometimes, you'll regress into old habits.

But you can remember this each time: you can pivot, breathe, and adapt.

You own a brand-new mental toolkit that no crisis can take away.

May you walk forward with lighter shoulders, a clearer mind, and a heart that's willing to embrace the fullness of life—the joys and the messiness alike.

May you stress less, love more, and dwell in the richness of every breath, every sunrise, every connection.

That, in itself, is a life well-lived.

A Personal Reflection

Before we close, let me share a small, personal reflection.

One morning, not too long ago, I woke up feeling oddly anxious for no discernible reason. My mind spiraled with "what-ifs." I'd just finished drafting one of these chapters the night before, and ironically, it was on cultivating peace.

I thought, *"What if I can't take my own advice? What if these are all just words?"*

But then I practiced a simple technique you'll find scattered throughout this book—mindful breathing. I inhaled slowly, counting to four, holding for a moment, and exhaled to a count of four—just that.

Within two minutes, my racing heart steadied. My swirling thoughts slowed enough for me to remember: *I'm allowed to feel anxious. It's just a feeling. And I have choices.*

That mini breakthrough reminded me that knowledge is powerless without practice.

I realized these concepts have to be lived, not just written about. And that's my final encouragement: *take these pages off the page.* Put them into practice in your own singular, messy, glorious life. Because you deserve that gift of a calmer mind and a brighter way of being.

Thank you for reading, learning, and, hopefully, living these words. May they serve as steadfast allies, reminding you at every turn that a life of mindful ease, purposeful connection, and ongoing evolution is possible and already unfolding within you.

And now, dear reader, I step aside. The spotlight is yours.

BIBLIOGRAPHY

Baer, R. A. (2003). Mindfulness training as a clinical intervention: A conceptual and empirical review. *Clinical Psychology: Science and Practice, 10*(2), 125–143.

>Explores the foundations of mindfulness interventions for stress reduction and details empirical support for their efficacy.

Brown, B. (2012). *Daring Greatly: How the Courage to Be Vulnerable Transforms the Way We Live, Love, Parent, and Lead.* Gotham Books.

>Offers insights into the power of vulnerability for emotional resilience and more authentic connections.

Cloud, H., & Townsend, J. (1992). *Boundaries: When to Say Yes, How to Say No to Take Control of Your Life.* Zondervan.

>Presents practical strategies for establishing healthier personal limits and reducing interpersonal stress.

Davidson, R. J., & McEwen, B. S. (2012). Social influences on neuroplasticity: Stress and interventions to promote well-being. *Nature Neuroscience, 15*(5), 689–695.

>Provides a scientific understanding of how chronic stress affects the brain and how targeted interventions can foster resilience.

Duckworth, A. (2016). *Grit: The Power of Passion and Perseverance.* Scribner.

>Examines how perseverance and "grit" underlie the capacity to persist through challenges, relevant to managing stress and building resilience.

Eisenberg, N. (2000). Emotion, regulation, and moral development. *Annual Review of Psychology, 51*, 665–697.

> Investigates how emotional regulation supports moral and empathetic behavior, enhancing well-being under stress.

Goleman, D. (1995). *Emotional Intelligence: Why It Can Matter More Than IQ*. Bantam Books.

> Introduces emotional intelligence as a vital predictor of stress management, relationship health, and personal success.

Gunaratana, H. (2011). *Mindfulness in Plain English*. Wisdom Publications.

> A user-friendly exploration of core mindfulness principles and practical application to daily stressors.

Kabat-Zinn, J. (2003). Mindfulness-based interventions in context: Past, present, and future. *Clinical Psychology: Science and Practice, 10*(2), 144–156.

> Summarizes the origins and scientific support for mindfulness-based stress reduction programs.

Kabat-Zinn, J. (2005). *Wherever You Go, There You Are: Mindfulness Meditation in Everyday Life*. Hyperion.

> Classic guide introducing simple meditative practices for coping with anxiety, busyness, and modern life pressures.

Kornfield, J. (2008). *The Wise Heart: A Guide to the Universal Teachings of Buddhist Psychology*. Bantam.

> Presents gentle, insightful approaches to reducing emotional turmoil and fostering compassion, drawn from Buddhist psychology.

Neff, K. (2011). *Self-Compassion: The Proven Power of Being Kind to Yourself.* William Morrow.

> Explores how offering kindness to oneself mitigates stress, anxiety, and burnout, fostering emotional well-being.

Neff, K., & Germer, C. (2018). *The Mindful Self-Compassion Workbook: A Proven Way to Accept Yourself, Build Inner Strength, and Thrive.* The Guilford Press.

> A practical workbook that underscores how blending mindfulness with self-compassion leads to profound stress reduction and inner resilience.

Seligman, M. E. P. (2011). *Flourish: A Visionary New Understanding of Happiness and Well-Being.* Free Press.

> Outlines the PERMA model—Positive Emotion, Engagement, Relationships, Meaning, Achievement—and its relevance to overcoming stress.

Segal, Z. V., Williams, J. M. G., & Teasdale, J. D. (2013). *Mindfulness-Based Cognitive Therapy for Depression.* The Guilford Press.

> Although focused on depression, this text offers insight into cognitive restructuring and mindfulness techniques that also alleviate stress.

Tolle, E. (2004). *The Power of Now: A Guide to Spiritual Enlightenment.* New World Library.

> A seminal exploration of present-moment awareness as a cornerstone for dissolving worry and emotional distress.

Viscott, D. (2014). *Emotional Resilience: Simple Truths for Dealing with the Unfinished Business of Your Past.* New Harbinger.

> Addresses how unresolved emotional baggage fuels ongoing stress, guiding readers toward practical ways to heal and move forward.

Ryan, R. M., & Deci, E. L. (2000). Self-determination theory and the facilitation of intrinsic motivation, social development, and well-being. *American Psychologist, 55*(1), 68–78.

> Investigates how fostering autonomy and intrinsic motivation improves mental health and stress outcomes.

Chiesa, A., & Serretti, A. (2009). Mindfulness-based stress reduction for stress management in healthy people: A review and meta-analysis. *The Journal of Alternative and Complementary Medicine, 15*(5), 593–600.

> Offers a research-based look at how MBSR programs effectively decrease stress symptoms in healthy populations.

Hofmann, S. G., Sawyer, A. T., Witt, A. A., & Oh, D. (2010). The effect of mindfulness-based therapy on anxiety and depression: A meta-analytic review. *Journal of Consulting and Clinical Psychology, 78*(2), 169–183.

> Explores empirical evidence showing that mindfulness-based interventions significantly reduce both anxiety and depression symptoms.

ADDITIONAL RESOURCES & PUBLICATIONS

Additional practical tips, *evidence-based articles*, and *interactive tools* to help readers integrate stress management seamlessly into their daily routines while cultivating emotional resiliency for the long haul

American Psychological Association (APA) – *Stress Management Resources*

> Comprehensive guides on everyday stress management, including step-by-step tips and free articles for developing coping skills.

www.apa.org/topics/stress

Mayo Clinic (2021) – *Stress Relief: Relaxation Techniques*

> Practical strategies and in-depth medical insights on implementing quick relaxation methods, with evidence-based overviews and patient-friendly exercises.

Anxiety & Depression Association of America (ADAA) – *Interactive Self-Help Tools*

> Offers worksheets, quick quizzes, and online programs designed for *instant anxiety relief* and building *emotional resilience.*

www.adaa.org

Mind Tools – *Everyday Stress Management Techniques*

> Focuses on short, practical tools such as the "ABCDE" method for rethinking anxious thoughts and brief on-the-go relaxation prompts.

www.mindtools.com/pages/article/newTCS_05.htm

Headspace App – *Guided Mindfulness & Quick Calming Exercises*

    Smartphone-based lessons on breathing, body scanning, and mindful breaks; also includes interactive sessions for high-stress moments.

www.headspace.com

Calm App – *10-Minute Relaxation & Instant Soothing Practices*

    Provides "emergency calm" sessions, daily mindfulness prompts, and sleep stories for anxiety and tension relief.

www.calm.com

PositivePsychology.com – *Free Mindfulness Worksheets & Resilience Articles*

    A hub of scientifically backed exercises and handouts covering acceptance, grounding techniques, and short resilience-building activities.

www.positivepsychology.com

Anxiety Canada – *My Anxiety Plan (MAP)*

    Structured CBT-based modules for learning everyday *stress management* skills, with interactive PDFs and videos.

www.anxietycanada.com

National Institute of Mental Health (NIMH) – *Featured Articles on Stress and Coping*

    Clear, research-oriented advice on immediate anxiety relief and routine stress reduction; frequently updated with new data.

www.nimh.nih.gov/health

"The Relaxation Response" (Herbert Benson, 2000)

> Seminal book detailing quick, evidence-based relaxation steps and the physiological underpinnings of stress relief. Encourages daily practice of a simple mind-body approach for *instant calming*.

"The 10-Minute Mind" (Monica Shea, 2022)

> Practical e-guide focusing on short, accessible mindfulness breaks, ideal for busy lifestyles seeking a daily *serenity boost*.

Mindfulness-Based Cognitive Therapy (MBCT) Online Programs – *Interactive Sessions*

> Digital courses blending CBT and mindfulness to quickly counteract negative thought spirals, bolster *emotional resilience*, and instill positivity.

Harvard Health Publishing – *Mind/Body Approaches for Stress Relief*

> Articles outlining how small daily habit changes—like progressive muscle relaxation or guided imagery—impact emotional health.

www.health.harvard.edu/topics/stress

Calm Clinic – *Instant Anxiety Tips*

> Internet resource offering quick-read articles for immediate tension reduction, panic attack coping tactics, and real-life success stories.

"The Little Book of Mindfulness" (Tiddy Rowan, 2014)

> Compact reference of bite-sized practices to calm the mind on the go, combining gentle reflections with user-friendly bullet points.

Mindful Self-Compassion Online Course – *Dr. Kristin Neff & Dr. Christopher Germer*

> Interactive digital modules emphasizing self-kindness, emotional regulation, and resilience-building, with hands-on home practices.

Stop, Breathe & Think App – *Customizable Meditation & Emotional Check-Ins*

> Users get short, curated sessions based on daily emotional states, facilitating *instant relief* and habit formation for calmer living.

"Real Happiness" (Sharon Salzberg, 2010)

> Includes a 28-day plan with structured, daily mindfulness exercises and journaling prompts that gently nurture a less reactive mindset.

Smiling Mind – *Free App & Lesson Plans*

> Australian not-for-profit providing interactive mindfulness programs for all ages, featuring short guided meditations for stress relief anywhere.

Therapy Aid "Relaxation Toolbox" – *Downloadable Worksheets & Tools*

> Offers fillable PDF forms, daily mindfulness checklists, and guidance on developing a personalized *stress management* routine.

ALSO BY THE AUTHOR

IF ONLY I HAD KNOWN, I WOULD HAVE DONE THINGS DIFFERENTLY
A Powerful Guide to Overcoming Regret, Making Better Decisions, and Living a More Fulfilling Life

RECLAIM YOUR BREATH, RECENTER YOUR HEART
An Essential Handbook for Habit Formation, Mental Clarity, and Emotional Balance

IN THE SERIES CLUELESS 101

NO-FUSS HOUSEKEEPING FOR THE TIME-STRAPPED
Low-effort Tips and Tricks that Actually Fit Your Life

SERVING LOVE, NOT PERFECTION—FIRST FAMILY DINNERS
How to make your Home (and your Heart) Shine

EMBRACE IMPERFECTION, FIND CONNECTION
Navigating New Romance with Ease

EMBRACE THE MESS, FIND YOUR FLAVOR
From Messy Mistakes to Mouthwatering Masterpieces

THE NOT SO DEFINITIVE JOYFUL GUIDE TO LOVING, LOATHING, AND LIVING
A Practical Guide to Life's Imperfections.

CALM CONVERSATIONS IN THE AIRS
A Holistic Guide to Overcoming Fear of Flying

Made in United States
Cleveland, OH
01 June 2025

17415990R00177